The Man Book: The Handbook for Men

15 Things a Man Needs to Know, Say, and Do

Tony Gaskins Sr.

The Man Book: The Handbook for Men

Copyright © 2015 by Tony Gaskins Sr.

All rights reserved. No part of this book may be reproduced or transmitted in any form or by any means without written permission of the author.

ISBN: 978-0692541180

Contents

The Creed of a Man．．．．．．．．．．．．．．．．．．．．．．．．．．．．．．1
Introduction．．．．．．．．．．．．．．．．．．．．．．．．．．．．．．．．．．．3

1 What Is Man: Becoming the Man in Me．．．．．．．．5
2 Responsibility: Responding to Your Ability．．．．．13
3 Relationships: Relating to Companionship．．．．．19
4 Husband: What It Takes to Love Your Wife．．．．．35
5 Fatherhood: The Most Important Job
   in the World．．．．．．．．．．．．．．．．．．．．．．．．．．．．．．．．．．43
6 The Role of Father to a Son: What to
   Teach Your Son．．．．．．．．．．．．．．．．．．．．．．．．．．．．．．．65
7 The Role of Father to a Daughter: What to
   Tell Your Daughter．．．．．．．．．．．．．．．．．．．．．．．．．．．．71
8 Stepfather: Another Step in Fatherhood．．．．．．．．83
9 Reputation: Recreation and Restoration．．．．．．．．85
10 Finances: Money Matters．．．．．．．．．．．．．．．．．．．．．．95
11 Good Credit: The Red Carpet or Black Top?．．．101

12 Driver's License: Pilot or Passenger?..........113
13 A Job: Production Line or President? 117
14 Transportation: Getting Where You
    Need to Go................................ 123
15 Diploma or GED: Get Your Papers 127

Note from the Author......................... 129
Dedication...................................131
Special Thanks................................133

The Creed of a Man

I am born a male, purposed to become a man.
To reach this goal, I must learn everything I can.
This isn't a journey, but rather a quest.
It will require a lot of me, and I will do my best.
There are things I must be mindful of along the way.
Like watching what I do, as well as what I say.
I must learn responsibility. I must walk in integrity.
I mustn't lie, I mustn't cheat, and I mustn't steal.
I must learn to be respectful to women,
and try to understand how they feel.
I must take full responsibility for all of my actions.
Which also means committing to others,
and not just my own self-satisfaction.
I must make sure I financially support and raise my children.
And when they have problems, be there to hear them.
To live the creed of a man is now my goal.
And I will accomplish it, with all of my mind,
heart, body, spirit, and, soul.

Introduction

HELLO AND WELCOME TO *THE Man Book: The Handbook for Men.* This is not a book of judgment; it is a tool to be used to help you be the best man that you can be and to pass it on to your son(s) for their son(s), and to your daughter(s) for their son(s).

To start with, men are made, not born. When God made the first man, Adam, He made him a full-grown man and put in him everything he needed to know, and also gave him wisdom beyond his knowledge, thus making him wise concerning matters he had not yet encountered. In other words, Adam came here fully loaded. With the exception of Eve, every other human being comes into this world as an empty, helpless infant, in need of being taught practically everything they need to know. It was the job of the man to teach those things. Needless to say, sin eventually separated the man from God's spiritual nurture, leaving him to his otherwise selfish nature.

A tadpole will automatically become a frog, and a caterpillar will automatically become a butterfly, but a boy will not automatically become a man. He will become an adult male, or a grown boy. Men still have to be made. But how can you teach what you haven't been taught? This book isn't to judge our fathers for what they didn't teach us, but rather to teach us so we will know and we will teach our sons and our daughters what our fathers didn't know to teach us. So without further ado, let's get started. (I pray that God blesses you with wisdom, knowledge, and understanding as you read this book.)

Chapter 1

What Is Man: Becoming the Man in Me

"What is man, that thou art mindful of him, and the son of man, that thou visit him?" (Psalm 8:4)

YESTERDAY'S MAN, TODAY'S MAN, AND tomorrow's man. These are the three subjects we're going to talk about in this chapter. Most of the people on this planet don't realize how big of a deal the man actually is, including the man himself. Did you know that man is the most valuable asset of all God's creations? Why? Because he's made in the image of God. God said, "Let Us make man in Our image..." (Genesis 1:26, KJV) Image is the likeness of somebody or something, it means to have all or most of the characteristics of a particular person or thing, therefore becoming a suitable example of them. Having God's characteristics is what defines us and makes us His superior creation.

Did you know that collectively man is the most dominant species on the planet? God said to them "… have dominion over the fish of the sea, over the birds of the air, and over every living thing that moves on the earth." (Genesis 1:28 NKJV) That meant putting man in charge of everything He made. As a result the man has tamed lions, tigers, bears, elephants, whales — the list goes on and on. Oh, by the way, that's where the man's controlling ways come from: The "dominion" (ruling power, authority, and "control") is in his nature. Did you know that because of his knowledge capacity and ability to build and figure things out, men collectively are the most intelligent species on the planet? The Lord said, "Behold they are one people (all in agreement), and they have all one language, and this is only the beginning of what they will do. And nothing that they propose to do will now be impossible for them." (Genesis 11:6ESV) That means anything man set his mind to do he will figure out a way to do it. As a result man has done everything he's put his mind to doing. Man has become presidents, doctors, lawyers, judges, engineers, architects, linemen, etc. He's built skyscrapers, airplanes, spaceships, submarines, etc. He's been to the moon, and is going to Mars. Whatever he has put his mind to, he has done it.

Did you know that the man is the head of the most dominant species on the Earth, which is the human race? "...the head of every man is Christ, the head of the woman is the man, and the head of Christ is God." (1 Corinthians 11:3 KJV) He placed you as the leader; when you don't lead, there are consequences. "Because you obeyed your wife and ate from the tree about which I commanded you, 'You must not eat from it,' cursed is the ground thanks to you; in painful toil you will eat of it all the days of your life." (Genesis 3:17 NET) Because God appointed you and placed the responsibility on you to lead your family, He expects you to do so. This doesn't mean for you not to listen to or consult your wife, He know that you don't have all the answers to every situation. Therefore there was a time when He said to Abraham "...What ever Sarah says to you, listen to her, ..." (Gen 21:12 HCSB) However it does mean that you are given the intuition to lead the family and the logic to assess the situation, and the responsibly to make the decision to get the needed result.

Did you know that men are the head of the family? "...as for me and my house, we shall serve the Lord." (Joshua 24:15 KJV) Did you know that God made you stronger? "Likewise, husband, live with your wives in an understanding way, showing honor to the woman as the weaker vessel ... that your prayers may not be hindered." (1 Peter 3:7 NEV) Did you know that

God gives the man the final say? " So the LORD God formed out of the ground every wild animal and every bird of the sky, and brought each to the man to see what he would call it. And whatever the man called a living creature, that was its name." (Genesis 2:19 HCSB) God intended for the man to make the call. God didn't even name Eve. "Male and female created He them; and blessed them, and called their name Adam in the day that they were created." (Genesis 5:2 KJV) God told the man to make the call, "Adam named his wife Eve because she was the mother of all the living." (Genesis 3:20 HCSB)

Now of course with this great power and authority came responsibility. "For unto whomsoever much is given, of him shall be much required…" (Luke 12:48 KJV) Since God has given you the authority over her, He requires you to treat her right. "… each one of you is to love his wife as himself, and the wife is to respect her husband." (Ephesians 5:33 HCSB) And as for the family He says, "Fathers, don't stir up anger in your children." (Ephesians 6:4 HCSB) As a man you also have the responsibly to provide for your family. "A good man leaves an inheritance to his children's children… (Proverbs 13:22 EVS) You also have the responsibility to raise them right. "Train up a child in the way he should go, and when he is old he shall not depart from it." (Proverbs 22:6 NKJV) This is where you repetitively teach your children good moral and ethical behaviors, so that they can go out into life and apply everything that you taught them and become successful. It should be every parent's goal that their children do better than they did. "…he who believes in Me, the works that I do he will do also; and greater works than these he will do…" (John 14:12 NKJV) That was yesterday's man, and his position, authority, duties, and responsibilities. However yesterday's man became distracted, neglectful, and redirected. He abandoned his position, authority, duties, and responsibilities, resulting in his sons becoming today's man.

Today's man is significantly different from yesterday's man. Most of today's men have mastered the virtual world, but have lost control of the real world. They are no longer doing the things that really matter. This breakdown is mainly due to the abandonment of the duties and responsibilities of the fathers' of yesterday's men. This means that yesterday's fathers failed to teach the position, authority, duties, responsibilities, morals, and ethics to their sons of today. Therefore many of today's men don't hold down jobs for extended periods of time, some don't even desire a job, and some just flat out will not work. Others of today's men have chosen to find women who are naive enough to take care of them. These are women whose fathers of yesterday didn't teach them the role of a man and not to take care of him. It's OK for a woman to hold down the fort if her man happens to be in a job transition; it's not OK for her to support a man who doesn't want to work. The Bible says, "... If anyone isn't willing to work, he should not eat." (2 Thessalonians 3:10 HCSB) Many of today's men have a child or several children that they don't really do anything for, or spend any time with. Then some of today's men who do spend time with their children are negative influences and counterproductive to them. It's because they do negative things in the presence of their children. It may be because they themselves weren't taught by their fathers how to represent themselves in the duties and responsibilities of a man. Well, it's time for today's man to start to read, listen, and learn how to become tomorrow's man. There are all sorts of information, infomercials, instructions, seminars, webinars — you name it, it's out there. Learn what you need to learn as today's man so you can become a better man today, and begin teaching your sons of today to be tomorrow's men.

Tomorrow's man is today's boy whose father taught him to cut the yard, which is teaching him work ethics. Tomorrow's man is today's boy whose father taught him the importance of good grades, which is teaching him intellectual ethics. Tomorrow's man is today's boy who saw his father show love and respect to his mother, which is teaching him relationship ethics. Tomorrow's man is today's boy whose father taught him the value of money, which is teaching him financial ethics. Tomorrow's man is today's boy whose father taught him to respect his sister, just because she was a female, which is teaching him chivalry ethics. Tomorrow's man is today's boy whose father taught him the importance of keeping his word, which is teaching him integrity ethics. Tomorrow's man is today's boy whose father taught him the characteristics of yesterday's man, which caused the boy to be a good, well-rounded man today. Now let's talk about some of the things tomorrow's man is made of.

Chapter 2

Responsibility: Responding to Your Ability

"I can do all things through Christ who strengthens me." (Philippians 4:13)

THE WORD RESPONSIBILITY IS A combination of two words, response and ability. Response is the physical reaction to a specific situation. Ability is the possession of the strength, means, or skills to do the required task. However, the ability to do something is worthless unless you actually do something. Therefore ability by itself is nothing, it only means you're able. It will stay nothing until it gets a response. When you respond, you get results. Therefore when you add response to ability, you get responsibility, which means responding with your ability, which is taking the appropriate action to resolve the situation. A grown man has the ability to do something about his situation; a responsible man actually does something about his situation. The reason most men are not responsible is because they're not responding. *Responsibility* is the foundation on which God made the man. Everything about being a real man revolves around responsibility, and even though there is a great deal of responsibility that comes with being a man, God built the man with the abilities and the resolve to appropriately fulfill those responsibilities. Responsibility is what converts the male into a man. A male man delivers packages; a responsible man delivers results. The sum of a responsible man is to build and maintain a strong family relationship with solid, wholesome values.

As a man you are capable of much more than you realize. What you're not, you can become. What you are doing that you shouldn't be doing, you can change. Responsibility is not just doing and being the things that you should do and be; it's also about not doing or being the things that you shouldn't be or do. It is also your responsibility to develop your character. Your character should consist of reliability, dependability, trustworthiness, and accountability.

There are two types of behaviors: instinctual, and learned. Instinctual are innate behaviors, or behaviors we are born with. Learned are behaviors we inherit through some type of teaching experience. Responsibility is a learned behavior, not instinctual, therefore, since we're not born with it, we have to be taught it, or learn it. In the first 18 years of your life, it is your parents' responsibility to instill in you the things that you need to know, do, and be in order to become a responsible, productive, and socially acceptable man. Since the man is the head of the family, the bulk of teaching that responsibility falls on him. However it's difficult to teach something that you yourself may not have been taught, and therefore don't know. In most cases, the fathers don't know how to teach responsibility because their fathers didn't know and therefore didn't teach them.

My mother was a great woman; my father, a very wise man. My mother died while I was very young and my father died when I had barely become an adult. My father and mother taught my nine brothers, two sisters, and me (the youngest) how to be men and women of integrity. I later realized that there was a lot more for me to learn. I taught my son and daughter a lot. I feel that I was and still am a good father. However I can look back and realize that there were some things that I didn't know and therefore couldn't teach my kids. In fact there were a lot of things that I didn't know, and didn't know that I didn't know. Then there were the things that I knew, but didn't expound upon enough. I didn't know that there are some things that you teach your kids that you need to reiterate, again and again. It is a father's duty to seek to learn responsibility. The problem back in the day was the lack of understandable and accessible information on becoming a man/father/husband. Nowadays there's a multitude of information available. So today it isn't a matter of "I wasn't taught," it's a matter of "Am I trying to learn?" Your father may have been absent, an addict, an alcoholic, or incarcerated. Maybe he was there, but not involved enough. In any case this is not about the faults of your fathers for what they didn't do. Because if you know what they didn't do, that means you know what you need to do. That responsibility now becomes yours. After all, it is your life and you are now an adult. That is what this is all about. Accepting, being, and teaching responsibility. It's the ultimate duty of every man to be responsible for his own, now grown life, and the lives of his dependents.

Responsibility consists of three parts: (1) discovery, (2) development, and (3) delivery. *Discovery* is learning all the things you are responsible for as a man. For example, you need to learn to understand women. They are always going to be a part of your life. So you need to understand what they need from you in the way of love, the things that are important to them, and the things they need to hear you say every now and then. Discover how important you are in your kids' lives, and their need for your love, support, and active involvement in their lives (all of your children). This means being dependable, available, reliable, and accountable. This also means disciplining yourself. Don't do things that can get you in trouble, or jail, like irresponsible drinking and driving, fighting, stealing, or drugs. Those are things that can get you thrown in jail, and hurt or affect everyone in your life.

Development is the process of change. It's doing the things you need to do to be what you need to be. Being accountable, being dependable, being available, and supportive, just to name a few. This can take some time and effort. Find a way to make the time you need to make, and put forth the effort that it takes in order to do what needs to be done. Some of the things will come easy and some will be hard. Just work at it until you get it, no matter how long it takes. Even if you are a grandfather, it still isn't too late to start.

The *delivery* is the result part of responsibility. It's the evidence of your efforts. It's when the people that matter can see a consistent and permanent change in your life. If you do these things you will become known as dependable, reliable, available, and supportive. To that I say awesome job.

Chapter 3

Relationships: Relating to Companionship

It's not good that man be alone. (Gen. 2:18)

ALLOW ME TO TELL YOU how a relationship normally goes, then how it should go. To do this let's fast-forward and look at a man's life at age 25–30. What we will find is that the average male would have had several relationships or sex partners, probably resulting in several children from the different women of these different relationships. In most of these cases the man isn't committed nor supportive financially or emotionally in the lives of the children or mother. In fact the man at this point is seeking yet another woman to become intimately involved with and possibly creating another child.

That scenario probably describes most men, which means that if this is common behavior throughout the male species, then there is a problem. Despite the common pattern, these men can be from different walks of life, yet doing the same things as it pertains to relationships. At the end of the day we are left with questions to which most men including some of you, don't know the answers. Questions such as why do we seek companionship? What initially got you into a relationship? Why do you continue to seek them? How do relationships affect the rest of your life? How does a relationship affect the other people involved? What went wrong? How do you make it right?

So, *why do we seek companionship*? Because we need companionship. Companionship is the presence and social interaction of another person(s). If a human being is raised without the social interaction of other human beings we would immediately begin a slow and painful emotional death. Ever notice how much a child desires physical interaction, to be held, carried, or cuddled? Scientific studies indicate that a baby never being held, talked to, cuddled, or comforted in any kind of way by a human would most likely cry itself to death in its infancy stage. The word of God says, "It is not good for the man to be alone..." (Genesis 2:18 HCSB) Studies also show that loneliness is also one of the greatest forms of punishment. For the children, they're placed in an area called time out, i.e. a room or wall facing away or isolating them from other kids. The adult version would be a prisoner being isolated from the rest of the inmate population by being placed in solitary confinement, also referred to as the box. We (man or woman) do not like being alone, and we were not made to be alone. Therefore we seek companionship. Companionship can be anyone — a relative, a friend, even a stranger. Companionship that's not biological can eventually leads to relationship.

What initially got you into a relationship? Obviously there are many different kinds of relationships. Relationships are defined by the way people are connected to one another. There are family relationships, friend relationship, neighbors, etc. The ultimate relationship is the intimate relationship between the man and the woman. The ultimate purpose of a relationship is sex. The ultimate purpose of sex is to reproduce. Adam and Eve were the first humans to be in a relationship, and if you notice they were made with the parts for reproduction right from the get go. So say what you want, every relationship that a man and a woman gets into is purposed to result in sex. It may not result in sex, but sex is the unpronounced or pronounced catalyst for the relationship. Sex is a deferred instinctual behavior in the man that seems insatiable once it is awakened. God genetically hardwired this desire and drive in your design from birth. Hardwired meaning it is the way God originally made the man starting with Adam. So the reason a man initially gets in to a relationship is because of his instinctual desire for sex. But this doesn't only apply to the man, it also applies to the woman. In fact is actually applies to every living thing that God created: dogs, cats, cattle, elephants, insects, plants, everything in the waters, even in the skies, even bacteria. God's universal commandment to every living thing in this universe is "be fruitful and multiply." (Genesis 1:28)

Let's take a look at how this reproductive instinct works, and at random let's select cattle for an example. The females of the cattle are called heifers if they have not had a mating experience. If the female has had a mating experience she is called a cow. The male cattle is called a bull; the young offspring are called calves. By God's design the cow will go into heat every 17–24 days (21 days on average). This means she is ready for a male to mate with her for the purpose of reproducing, euphemistically speaking; in other words she's ready for sex. During this time she will literally seek a male and make herself available for the male when she finds one. During this period her normal behavior will change. She will moo a lot more than normal, she doesn't want to sleep, she becomes aggressive, irrational, and even unpredictable. If there are no bulls around she will go through mating motions with other females. However, when she finds the bull or the bull finds her, she doesn't just give it up, she makes him work for it. She goes through two basic stages, walking heat and standing heat. In the walking heat she makes him literally chase her for 10 to 18 hours straight. She walks and walks around the herd, throughout the pasture, around in circles, where ever she spontaneously decides to go. He has to relentlessly keep up with her. If he doesn't keep up, or can't keep up, he loses his opportunity to mate with her. She is making him prove his worthiness. When he has proven himself and she is ready, she will then proceed into the standing heat. This is when she decides to stand still and allow him to mate with her. Once she conceives, she's done. She doesn't go into heat again, she doesn't let another bull mate with her, she proceeds to prepare to deliver the calf. With some variations, this type of instinctual mating repeats itself throughout the different species, and all for the purpose of reproduction. Now, there is a problem. When a man's body starts this reproductive phase (goes through puberty), he doesn't really understand it and therefore doesn't know how to properly channel it. His mind and sexual drive aren't in sync. In other words, his sexual hormones are saying *let's reproduce*, but the message reaching his brain is simply saying *sex, sex, sex, and more sex*. That sex drive in the man doesn't turn off like it does in the other species. The bull we just spoke about identifies the female by smell. He is able to smell her pheromones from some distance away, from which he becomes sexually stimulated. The man on the other hand is able to see women from some distance away, from which he is sexually stimulated. The bull by smell, the man by sight. Every time the man sees an attractive woman, he becomes sexually stimulated by the sight of that particular woman. His body tells his brain that they need to work her, so he does like the bull and begins to do everything he can to sex her. If he is in the store, he will anticipate her travels and try to position himself in the right place to converse with her. Often times he will be successful and these encounters may result in a relationship. Because he doesn't know how to channel his sexual desire (which we will discuss later in this chapter) he continues to pursue other women that he finds himself sexually attracted to even while already in a relationship. As a result he may produce multiple offsprings from some of the different women he encountered.

Why do you continue to seek relationships? The real reason is because you continue to want sex, but not willing to do what you really need to do to stay in the relationship that you get in. So the relationship ends. It could have ended due to a number of reasons, you lost interest, you felt like she became too needy, or too clingy. She was ready to take it to the next level and you weren't. You chose not to accept the responsibility that relationships evolves to, but most likely you got caught cheating. But no matter what the reason for your last relationship ending, in the end you still don't want to be alone, so you continue to seek relationships even if you're the reason they continue to fail.

Why do men cheat? Most of the time it's simply because you saw someone else you found sexually attractive and you went for it. It's not that there was anything wrong with the woman you was already with, you was just sexually attracted to the other woman you saw.

How do the relationships affect the rest of your life? Men get into relationships based on their sexual desire or attraction to a woman. It may have been just a pretty face or a fine body. But selfish sex can lead to a pregnancy, and part-time loving can easily turn in to a full-time child. A child and its mother are forever, even if the child is not living with you and you're not married to her. No child deserves the isolated feeling of being raised without a father. And no woman deserves to suffer undue mental and emotional pain and have her body suffer sometimes unrecoverable physical changes just for being attractive. I know that we may not have realized these things when we did them, but what we need to do now is try to make them right. You've changed the life of that/those women forever, and it's only right that yours changes to. <u>So many men think of a child as 18 years of child support. The fact of the matter is that they need support in their adult lives too, they need life support.</u>

How do relationships affect the other people involved? It can be positive or negative, but most of the time it's negative. Why? Because relationships usually produce children, and if the father fails to be involved (which happens a lot) the child can grow up without proper guidance, which can lead to a troublesome life. They may grow up resentful, rebellious, in and out of trouble, in and out of jail. All because they felt rejected and neglected of a love they needed — your love. As for the mothers that experienced these pregnancies in which the man later broke off the relationship, they may develop abandonment and trust issues and carry these damaged emotions into their future relationships, which can cause those relationships to fail therefore affecting them for a long time if not a lifetime.

So what went wrong? It starts as teenagers. The male hormones began to go wild, causing his body instinctively to begin to desire a female for the purpose of sex. This desire produces his rap game and his approach. He hones his game with each female that he approaches. What seems right to him is actually wrong for her. He presents himself driven by instincts coupled with learned behaviors. He display a genuine interest, flattery, compliments, and sincerity; a combination that a woman finds hard to resist and it usually gets him what he wants. He will repeat this display of interest and affection to the very next attractive female that peaks his sexual desire. Since he is competitive by nature, he's purposed to get her before the next man does and will even tries to woo her from him if she's already with him. He will present himself as willing to give her more of whatever she wants, actions he has no real intentions of keeping. This is simply the actions of the self-taught young male instinctively doing whatever it is that he needs to do to get what his relentless nature is desiring. The desire will continue to repeat every time he sees an attractive woman. Of course he will not succeed every time, but it will not be due to a lack of trying.

Without being properly told what is happening with his body, and what he must do to control this seemingly uncontrollable desire, he will continue to get with as many females as he possibly can, and this will carry over well into his adult life. At this point he's not considering the consequences of his actions, just trying to get more action. Also at this point he's not really too interested in putting in the work to make a relationship work, except for the sexual benefits.

How do you make it right? To start with the man would need to take a little time and learn something about himself from his maker. We weren't supposed to be out looking for sex, we are supposed to be out looking for relationship. God said we're made in His image, and we discussed that earlier. What that mainly meant is that we have his characteristics. The bible declares God as an "Author and Finisher". (Hebrews 12:2 KJV) An author is a person who originated or gave existence to something. Originate is the origin in which something started or began. It's in our nature to start or begin something. If you notice, we usually always accost (approach) the female. That's the beginning of the relationship. We end up getting her pregnant; that's beginning a family. But as men we are also stigmatized by women as always starting something but hardly ever finishing it. That just happens to be more true than not. However God did not intend for the man to behave as animals that have no moral or ethical standards of obligation. In other words, it's OK for the male gender of animals to reproduce a lifeline and abandon it as many of them do, but we're not of the animal kingdom. God made the man with the expectation and wherewithal to build a lifelong relationship with the mate of his offspring, to stay with her and complete the process which he started "For the woman who has a husband is bound by the law to her husband as long as he lives..." (Romans 7:2 NKJV) So contrary to our nature, by design we are authors and finishers. Builders and fixers, our jobs are to build a good relationship, and when something goes wrong, fix it. Don't go start another family. Finish what you started.

How do relationships develop? All relationships, whether initiated by the male or the female, have three basic stages: visual, emotional, and physical. Each stage has a two-step process: indulgence and transition. As the two people indulge further into each stage, that particular stage transitions to the next stage. The visual stage is an observational stage. Before a relationship starts there has to be some interest between the two people. This interest usually starts when the two people visually inspect one another. Once they see the features that they find attractive in the other person, they then began communicating. As their communication increases so do their feelings for each other. Once their feelings increase to a certain point, then emotions begin to evolve; it then transcends to the emotional stage. When their emotions reach their peak the emotional stage transcends to the physical stage, which is the sexual stage. It's very important that we allow each stage to properly mature before moving to the next. The process is actually a little different for the male. The male enters relationships as a two-stage process: visual and physical. He basically eliminates the emotional stage by replacing it with an accelerated physical stage. The woman doesn't know this because the physical stage has lots of emotional characteristics. But the emotional stage is the most important stage because it actually develops the characteristics that determine the longevity of the relationship. It has expectations, requests, demands, and needs, all of which are very important to the woman and should be for the man as well. But for the male the physical stage is the dominating stage and the catalyst for him getting into relationship. The man because of his seemingly uncontrollable sexual desire often repeatedly finds himself in trouble. Simply because if he sees an opportunity to get involved with someone he finds sexually attractive he will, even if he's currently in a relationship or marriage. When he gets caught cheating, he will go to extreme measures to reestablish his relationship/marriage. Once he's back in it, he may likely repeat those actions several more times before he stops. Sometimes that significant relationship may end before his unfaithful actions do. So, should "we" (men), be held accountable for our actions now that it's apparent that this problem derives from an innate instinctual behavior? Will God hold man accountable for his infidelity, even though He seemingly made him this way? The answer: Yes, He is holding him accountable. We are still responsible for our actions because it is our responsibility to learn how to control our instinctual behaviors. The Word of God says "...to whom much is given, much will be required." (Luke 12:48 NKJV) God has given the man authority over everything on the face of the Earth, and of course that includes himself.

Can I change my sexual instincts? Yes, our lives would be quite inadequate if we only lived by instinctual behaviors, seeing how they are impromptus of the homeostasis and peripheral nervous system, whose basic functions are primal means of survival. So in order to have a normal, comfortable, productive, and even pleasant life, you must incorporate "learned" behaviors, which means behaviors you're going to have to learn. We actually should develop ourselves to a point so that all of our normal, everyday functions and activities are controlled by learned behaviors. A big part of those learned behaviors has to be learning how to do right as it pertains to sex and relationships. This happens to be a very hard thing for us men to do, but not impossible. We are very capable of learning, and we can become very good at what we learn. We've been learning all of our lives, ever since the day we were born. We grow up learning that there are rules and laws that we must obey. These also become the rules of life. Rules or laws are put in place to protect rights, life, and property. A violation of a rule or law is an infringement of someone's rights and there are consequences for those violations. As men, we are competitive by nature. We compete in basically everything we do. We learn that there are even rules by which we compete. Even in this "game of life" as some call it, if you're going to compete or be successful at it, you have to learn the rules that apply to it. For example, if you're going to play football, you have to learn the rules for football. If you want to play basketball, then you have to learn the rules for basketball, which are different from football. The same goes for baseball, boxing, hockey, and so on. We also learn what is called "good sportsmanship." Good sportsmanship is the belief that a sport or activity will be enjoyed for its own sake with proper consideration for *fairness, ethics, and respect.* <u>From boys to men we learn to show sportsman-like-conduct as respect for the game, now it's time we learn to show gentleman-like-conduct as respect for the woman.</u> Because even though you might not see a referee on your playing field to throw a flag, eventually foul plays will be reviewed (exposed) and penalties will be accessed (a breakup).

Can a man do right? If he chooses to. He can do whatever he wants to do — we established that in the first chapter. I'm not even talking about being abstinent from sex. Paul says you should try to abstain like himself, but if you can't then "But if they do not have self-control, let them get married, For it is better to marry than to burn with sexual desire." (I

Corinthians 7:9 NET) Your body may instinctually need sex, which of course will be with a woman. But it doesn't instinctually need sex form every woman. You can do right by choosing to do right. Before you get in a relationship, decide that you're going to find one woman that you are attracted to, and be faithful to her. Then when you establish that relationship with her, continue to choose to be faithful to her. You're going to see plenty other fine women, but remind yourself that you're in a relationship and that you're going to be faithful to her. Is it going to be hard to do, maybe so, but so is football, boxing, basketball, etc. You can do it.

Chapter 4

Husband: What It Takes to Love Your Wife

Husband, love your wives, even as Christ loved the church, and gave himself for it; (Ephesians 5:24)

O NE OF THE BIGGEST DECISIONS a man will ever make in his life is when he decides to become a husband. Marriage is the ultimate stage of relationship, and the ultimate expression of commitment. The wedding band, which symbolizes an unending love, is also the man's continual voice that's saying, "I have made my choice, I am in love and committed to a very special lady." People can secretly be in a relationship, but a marriage requires witnesses. For those ladies that didn't get an invitation, the ring is the indication. You can walk away from a relationship anytime you choose; marriage requires permission. Marriage is a legal knot tied willingly and on purpose to help hold you together during the rough and tough times, and all marriages need help at some point or another. Relationship allows you to still be your own boss; marriage requires co-management. Relationship allows you to live apart; marriage brings you together.

I'm not going to stay in this chapter too long. This particular advice is like saving bonds — the longer you've been married, the more valuable it is. So here are a few things you will need to know. There's going to come a time sooner or later when your wife is going to say to you or ask you "Do you still love me?" "You don't treat me like you use to," "You hardly talk to me anymore," and a number of other things. Now, of course you're going to disagree with her and tell her that you do still love her. But that's just going to lead to a number of other long, inconclusive, and unresolved conversations. Unfortunately these conversations are going to be periodically repeated. One way to resolve this is to pay attention to what she's saying and agree to work on the things that need to be worked on. This will mean you telling her more often that you love her, and doing things to show her. But chances are you won't keep this up, and the conversations will resume. When all else has failed, you may have to try explaining to her that a man may not continue to engage a woman with the same intensity that he initially pursued her with, but that doesn't mean he loves her any less. It really is the truth, even though you might have promised her that you wouldn't change, that you would always love her the same. The truth is the intensity doesn't stay the same, but that doesn't mean that your love has actually changed. But listen, you will have to step up your game, after all she is telling you how she feels because it's how she is really feeling. If she continues to feel like this, she will eventually become vulnerable, which can ultimately lead to an indiscretion. Her telling you this is her way of crying out. It's also her way of warning you that she's becoming vulnerable. She is not threatening you, instead it's her sincere way of making you aware. So you really need to makes some changes, mentally and physically make yourself give her more attention. She needs compliments, and she needs attention. After all, that's how you got her in the first place, and that's how God made her. So although it's not necessary to do it all the time, you are going to have to do it more often than you were before this conversation between you and her took place. So you have to change, or at least, make some changes.

Your wife will also need you to be a friend, not a boss nor a father, but a friend: someone she can talk to, someone who will listen. Actually you're going to be a sounding board. She doesn't actually need you to talk much during her sounding board sessions, but she does want to know that you're listening. She needs you to be a part of her social emotional support system. Women love to talk and might be on the phone a lot with another woman friend. In the beginning it's going to seem like she's on the phone too much, but after some time in the marriage, you might actually be glad when she's on the phone. But her main social sounding board will be you. You're going to hear about everything that's going on all around her at work, on Facebook, on her side of the family, and so on. The main thing you have to do is just be a supportive listener and give some occasional comments. But make sure those responses are definitely in your wife's favor. Do not, I repeat, do not try to fix the things she is talking about. By nature we are fixers. But what we fix are cars, houses, and other things like that, and we're better off sticking to fixing those things. Do not try to fix the issues that she always wants to tell you about. For example, take that female co-worker or that female so-called work friend that she talks about almost every day. Naturally you're going to fix it. You're going to say something like, "She's not a friend, you don't even need to be talking to her," "She did what? Isn't she married? I don't want her ever coming around here!" Next thing you hear they are still going out to lunch together.

But the thing is she doesn't want you to fix what she's telling you, she just wants you to listen. Even though it will be hard for you to do, the best thing for you to do is just listen and keep your responses limited to things like "What, you got to be kidding me," "Really," "What in the world was she thinking?" "She is a trip," etc. The things you really want to say, keep them to yourself. You stay there and you'll stay safe. Get anymore involved, and you and you wife are going to be in an argument, and you'll end up saying, "Don't tell me anything else about your work." But she needs to talk about it, and she want to talk to you about it, so it's best to try to learn to listen a lot, and say a little.

Become a listener. That's harder for a man than it sounds. The only way we learn what we need to know about her and what's important to her is by listening to her. For starters, before you get married you will learn if an actual wedding is or isn't important to her. Most women it is, but to some it isn't. To most men it's a waste of money, to most women it's the crown of their relationship. By listening we learn what colors she likes, the type of earrings, and the style of jewelry she likes. (Just knowing those things is more important than you may think.) Listen to her ideas, her views, and her opinions because they have emotional waves attached to them. Sometimes she is going to be very happy with ideas and things she would like for y'all to do or plan to do. Don't be too quick to fix it; in other words, don't be too quick to deconstruct it. We have to learn to put our rational or logical nature aside sometimes. Otherwise you're going to shut down almost everything she says, and she's going to end up telling you how irrelevant she feels in "your" marriage, and how what she thinks, feels, or says doesn't matter. Instead, you should probably say, "OK let's think about it, and we'll talk some more about it later." But if you really consider them, you'll actually find that some of the things make good sense, besides you're going to have to do some of it anyway for the sake of peace. You've heard it before, "Happy wife, happy life."

Pay her more attention. There's going to come a time sooner or later that this is going to become an important conversation. Not getting enough attention. This is super important! I'll say it again, if women were ever to cheat, this would most likely be why she would say she did it: the overwhelming feeling of chronic neglect. Lack of attention usually never happens in the beginning of the relationship. It's usually at least a year, or perhaps two years into the relationship. When she complains about a lack of attention, she isn't necessarily talking about sex. At this point, she's complaining that you don't show her enough affectionate attention. She's complaining that you don't touch her like you used to. She will say that she wants you to touch her more, not necessarily in a sexual manner, but by holding her hand, sometimes putting your arm around her while you all walk in the store, or from the car to the restaurant. She wants you to touch her at times and in ways that are not followed by sexual relations. That makes her feel that you are still in love with her and not just waiting until you are ready to have sex before you touch her.

There's a scripture that says "….and the two shall become one flesh." (Genesis 2:24) The word flesh means physical persons, and becoming one, means to be agreed. So "the two become one flesh" means the two of you reaching a place of agreement on whatever it is that you're discussing or debating. To make a marriage work, the husband and wife are going to have to "learn" to walk in agreement. This doesn't mean that you and her are going to agree on everything. There are going to be some things that y'all are going to have to agree to disagree on. However, you both still really need to reach agreements, even if they are compromised agreements.

Chapter 5

Fatherhood: The Most Important Job in the World

ANY MAN CAN BE THE father of a child. The question is, will he be a father to the child? I'm going to ask you some questions and I would like for you to record the answers on a piece of paper or on your electronic device. In assessing (not judging) your father, what things do you wish he would have done, done more of, or not done, in your life? Take your time and thoroughly answer those questions. Once you have completed the questions, the answers will become your foundation as a father for your kids. Make sure that you do enough of the things you wish your father had done, and don't do any of the things you wish he hadn't done. That's just for starters.

I heard a story many years ago. It was about a man who wanted to change his life, get a new lease on life so to speak. A friend in another state bought him a train ticket and told him to come out there, said it would be a great place to restart. In the course of travel, the attendants passed out menus to all the passengers and told them they would be back around to take their orders. During their conversation after the friend picked up the man from the train station, the friend commented on how good the food is on that particular train, and asked the man which meal he chose, the chicken or the steak, stating that both were great. "I didn't order either, I didn't have any money," the man said. The friend shockingly replied, "But it was included in the price of the ticket!" "I didn't know," said the man.

The Word of God says, "My people are destroyed for a lack of knowledge." (Hosea 4:6 ESV) You would be surprised at the things people don't do or don't get just because they don't know. You would also be surprised at the things people don't get because they didn't ask. "…yet you have not, because you ask not." (James 4:2 KJV) These people I'm talking about who didn't do or get anything, it's because their parents didn't teach them that. For one reason or another, the parents didn't tell or teach their children about preparing, inquiring, or ascertaining beneficial information. Let's just say it was because the parents didn't know. So I'm telling you this so that you will know to begin searching right now so that you can learn all you can to teach your children. You may or may not have gone to college. You may or may not be a prominent man in our society. You may or may not have a good or high-paying job. Whether you have or have not it's OK, because this chapter isn't about what you have or have not done for yourself, it's about what you have done, can do, and will do, for your children. So you might not have gone to college but you can do what you need to do to make sure your children go to college. You might not be a prominent man, but you can do what you need to do to get your children on the right path to become prominent. Keep in mind this is about you, not your children's mother; mothers do what they can do, but they can't do what you can and are supposed to do.

Men sometimes have the mentality that the boy should be their responsibility to raise, and the girl should be the responsibility of the mother. A woman only has half (23 chromosomes) of what it takes to make a child, the man has the other half (23 chromosomes). When the woman is impregnated by the man, that means his 23 chromosomes have paired off with her 23 chromosomes, making a child consisting of 23 chromosomes. Notice that the child does not consist of 46 chromosomes, but 23, because each one of his chromosomes infuses itself with each one of her chromosomes, and their 2 chromosomes become 1. So their 46 chromosomes became 23 pairs. Therefore every child, regardless of whether it's a girl or a boy, consists of 23 parts of their father and 23 parts of their mother. It is imperative that each parent raises their part of each child. The boy needs his mother and the girl needs her father, the boy needs his father and the girl needs her mother, from an infant through its adolescent stages until he or she becomes a full-grown adult.

It's a man's nature to be in control; we are also builders and fixers. Well, as a father this is your chance, your time, in fact it's your job to take control of your child's life and build it to be the best man or woman they can be. I'm not going to kid you and say it's not a challenging job because there is a lot to being a father to your children. You may not even know how to be a good father; if you don't then the first part of your job is to learn. This book is going to be of help and there are many more self-help tools out there.

If I ask you whether your father was a good father, whether he was supportive of your extracurricular activities, spent a lot of time with you, had beneficial talks with you, was a good role model, was a man of his word, and taught you what you needed to know to be a good man, you are going to be able to answer every one of those questions, and it's going to be your own answer; no one, not even your mother, will be able to influence the answers. To the fathers of grown children, you will be surprised to hear some of the things your kids will have to say about you; some of the things will be downright embarrassing for you. Some of your children are going to say you were, "no good," "not there for them," "a liar," "a drunk," "a cheater," etc. They will say whatever they know. For you young fathers who are in the process of raising your children, keep all of this in mind.

If you have sons, did you or are you teach(ing) them all they need to know (about finances, about being fair in relationships, about being responsible, what can make them successful, etc.) to be a well-rounded man? I'm not talking about thinking or hoping they figure it out; did you teach them? If you have daughters, did you or are you teach(ing) them all they need to know (about finances, about men, about relationship, about responsibility, about success) to be well-rounded women? If not then learn what you need to learn so you can teach them. If your children are grown, there are still things you can teach them.

You may say, "What is my part? What am I to do? What am I to instill in my children?" As a father you're not only very important, but your role in your children's lives is devastatingly important. Your role has three parts. The first is your general role as father to your son(s) and daughter(s) teaching them the general things that children need to be taught. Second is your specific role to your son(s). Your son(s) are going to be men one day. As you know men are different from women. Therefore, you have to teach him things that only pertain to him as a male. Third is your specific role to your daughter(s). Likewise, you have to teach your daughter things that she needs to know and do as it pertains to dealing with men.

Let's also talk about your children who do not live with you. There are many men who have children being raised by their mothers, whom they are no longer with. These children still need their father to do his part in their lives. It's obvious that you're not going to be in their lives as much as you would be able to be if they lived with you. But they need you to be there for them nonetheless, so you must do your part. You can do this by getting court-appointed dates and times to get your children. The reason for doing this has nothing to do with whether or not you and your children's mother are having problems. Instead this is a method to help you establish a routine for seeing your children. Without doing this, you may be less likely to get them on a regular, consistent basis.

The second thing you need to do is establish some child support. Yep, child support. Work out a fair amount of child support that you can do and be consistent with it. Notice I said a fair amount that you can do, I didn't say a fair amount that you can pay.

Why? Because paying is actually just a small part of child support. Being a father is much more than that. To find out what "more" you can do, let's take a closer look at the words child support. The child part is quite obvious. So let's take a closer look at the word support and its definition. Support is (1) *to be present,* (2) *to give active help,* (3) *to encourage,* (4) *to support financially,* (5) *to give assistance,* (6) *to comfort,* (7) *and to reinforce.* That's what support is. So then what is child support? Child support is to support your child in all seven of these ways, and I could have named more. So then, what is "paying" child support? "Paying" child support is only one of the seven means of support that you are to give your child. Although it is very necessary, very important, and very much your responsibility to "pay" the financial part of the child support, the sad truth of the matter is that most men wouldn't even be paying what they are paying if it weren't for the court system. In fact, even with an order from the courts, many men still don't pay child support, or they pay only enough to stay out of jail. My appeal to you as men is to pay all of your child support. By not paying your child support you're not beating the system or your child's mother; what you're actually doing is cheating your child. I know how guys think, *Why should I give her money and she is sleeping with some one else?* That particular child would not be here in this world if it were not for you. That is your seed, from your sperm. That child is literally you, yours, and you are the one who should be taking care of him/her. Men seem to think that they are taking care of their child's mother with the money that they pay for the child. Or they are overly concerned about what the child's mother does with the money. Well, your child's mother also supports him/her financially as well. Not only does she support your child financially, but also emotionally, morally, physically, and a whole lot more; not to mention that she also does all of this every single day. So when you don't pay your child support, you're telling your child that you're not willing to help feed or clothe or do whatever your money is needed to do. You may be one of the few men who do pay their child support. If so, to you I say "well done," and I encourage you to encourage your brethren to pay their child support also. As I said earlier, this is only the financial part of the support, which is one out of seven things you are supposed to be doing. Let's take a brief look at the other six areas of child support that you are also supposed to be doing.

(1) Being present. This one is the most important of them all. It's the foundation. This means to be there and to actually be a physical presence throughout your child's entire life. It means spending time with your children (all of them), the ones who live with you, and the ones who don't. To be present means to

buy them gifts and spend time with them for their birthdays and for Christmas. It means to be at their extracurricular activities, such as baseball, football, cheerleading, basketball, gymnastics, etc. It really means being there and not just saying you will, and then you don't show up. It means doing what you say, not calling afterward and apologizing. If your job schedule conflicts with these events, communicate this with your child. Find out when their big or important events are (it's important to them), then switch out those dates in advance, and be present. Sometimes you just need to make sacrifices for your children. It'll make memories they'll never forget. Oh, by the way, if you're not there, it will still make memories they won't forget. So do your best to be a good father, and be there.

(2) To give active help. This may come later in their lives, but this is also very important. This means to be there in their times of need, to really be there and help them through whatever situations they are going through. This means being a father they feel comfortable and confident to talk to during these times. You will need to have already established this comfort and confidence. (We'll talk that about that shortly.) They sometimes need advice or may need you to speak for them even as young adults, because things are going to arise that they are just not going

to be experienced enough to handle. So if they need you, be there to help them.

(3) Encouraging them. As a father, it is important to encourage your children. This starts as early as tee-ball, or the Little League experience. Encourage them to keep playing when they want to quit. This need for encouragement may be necessary at several points in their lives. Encourage them to do what's right, whatever that might be. Encourage your children to make mature and sound decisions. Encourage them to trust and follow their hearts, and their good minds. Encourage them through their hard times, encourage them through their failures, through their low points in life, and even through their bad decisions. We all need encouragement sometimes in our lives. Be there for them.

(5) Assisting them. Let your children know that you're there for them to help them with their young adult life transition. Do whatever things you can to assist (help) them on their journey. They may need you to keep your grandkids some days or nights while they complete a class, obtain a degree, a trade, etc., in an effort to better themselves. They may need your assistance in organizing their home or a budget. It's about being available to them and for them.

(6) Comforting them. Sometimes unfortunate things can happen in our kids' lives, so establish a close enough relationship with your kids that you

know what's going on with them. These misfortunes may come in the form of a loss of some sort or another. It can be as simple as the loss of a game that's important to them or the loss of a job, a car, a house, a friend, a significant other, or anything. When your kids do experience things that hurt them, empathize with their situation. Their mother is usually always there for them, so they would love to know that their father also cares about what really matters to them too.

(7)Finally, reinforce them. Your kids need reinforcement. This means re-instilling the things that you have already taught them, like being strong, confident, responsible, independent, resourceful, being sure of who they are, and even being encouraged. Again these are things you've already taught them. Now you're just taking them to the next level, making sure they will be the best that they can be by doing the best they can do. Remember, you don't want to disable your children by doing everything for them. Instead you want to enable them by having them do what you taught them to do which is to stand on their own two feet and to be the man, woman, father, mother, wife, and husband you've taught them to be. Ask anyone who has raised children from infancy to adulthood and they can attest to the fact that you are definitely going to face some worries, concerns, and situations that you have no idea how to handle.

But don't put any undue pressure on yourself to be a super dad. Just learn all you can and try to be the best dad you can be.

Let's talk some about raising children from infancy through adolescence and to adulthood. As we have just discussed, the first role you take on is the role of support. Don't worry about trying to teach anything in the beginning. Your kids will first go through about five phases: (1) adjusting, (2) observing, (3) exploring, (4) creating, and then (5) maintaining. You simply help them out by accommodating, assisting, and teaching them through each phase.

Take for example the *adjusting phase*. This is the phase where the infant child begins making his/her adjustments to their new environment and new world. At this stage very little observing, exploring, creating, or maintaining is going to be done. This is about making adjustments. For the first time in their entire life, they have just experienced their first physical separation from their mother. The child is now adjusting to this new cold hospital room, rather than momma's warm 98.6-degree body temperature. And breathing and eating through their nose and mouth, rather than in utero from mom's umbilical cord. In this stage there's going to be lots of eating, sleeping, bowel movements, eating, sleeping, bowel movements, eating, sleeping, bowel movements, then more eating, sleeping, and bowel movements.

The next phase is the *observatory phase.* At birth the newborn can only see about 6–12 inches, everything else is fuzzy. However at about 7 months, the infant's eyesight is as good as yours. The observatory phase is when children start to visually inspect their new environment. You will see many expressions of amazement and expressions of study. It's also amusing and elating as you take them on walks through the house and watch them muse over the things they see. It doesn't really matter what they're looking at because everything is new to them. You will however notice that some things catch their attention more than others. You'll also find these walks to be quite useful during times when your child is crying due to what may be determined as an unsettling or disquieting mood, due to something other than being hungry or in need of a diaper change.

Then they transition to the *exploring phase.* That's the stage where they are crawling really well or walking. It's here when they start to get into literally everything. This is where you really need to watch them and keep them safe by governing what they can and can't do. This is also where you start to teach them to listen and obey with voice commands. But keep in mind they are just kids, so you must have plenty of patience and remember that their exciting and intriguing new discoveries and curiosities are much more interesting and alluring than the words "no," "stop it," or "come here." This exploring phase, which entails curiosities, as well as many new discoveries to investigate, can last well in to their adulthood. But next it takes us to what is known as those terrible twos.

Now this is really when some corrective action needs to start. At this stage, a good, stern, firm, precise voice is all you need. Not a belt, switch, or heavy hand, but a voice. This is really where we also see how important the father is. As you may know, a woman is made or designed for nurturing and caring for children. Her sense of hearing is heightened to pick up high-pitched sounds. This is so she will hear and respond to her infant's cry, or distress call, even if she's in a deep sleep. She was also given a softer voice than the man. So the sound of her voice is comforting and soothing to her infant/child. Her voice is so comforting, soothing, and less frightening that her kids later begin to ignore it. This is when that more fearful voice of the man comes into play. Most all parents go through that stage when it takes everything the mother has to get the child to listen to her, and the dad can just say something one time and without raising his voice, and the child will obey. You just speak using a clear, direct, stern, and firm voice; you don't even need to yell or get angry. Your voice will be sufficient. However, in time you will need to use some voice inflections.

Responsibility as we discussed earlier, is the foundation for a man. As fathers it's the most important thing that we can teach our children. It is the glue that holds everything else together. The teaching of concrete responsibility can begin as early as 2 years of age. You can start by designating a container as the toy box (storage) and having your children put their toys back in the toy box once playtime is over. Children will throw candy wrappers, cups, etc. on the floor when they're finished with them. Teach them to pick up whatever they have thrown down and put it in the trash. When they get a little older, give them chores around the house and have them do their chores consistently. Then when they get even older put them in extracurricular activities, such as football, cheerleading, basketball, piano lessons, etc. This is where you begin to teach them the greatest part of responsibility, which is not quitting. This teaches them to complete what they start. When they are young it's OK for you or their mother to choose their activities for them. Or if they have an interest in something and you feel it's appropriate, then let them do it. You will find that kids have short attention spans. They also have a short-term interest in the activities that they or you choose for them. Again the key to responsibility is not quitting. So it's important that you talk to them, encourage them, and support them, but don't let them quit (at least not until they have completed that season or course of that particular activity).

Now, let's talk about disciplining. Men, please do not beat your children. When I say beat, I mean do not beat them with a belt, or with a stick, or your heavy hands. Most of the time, men beat the kid with an intention for them to know that they just got their behinds tore up. I know that many of you are reflecting on the spankings (or beatings as we called them back in the day) that you got when you were a child, and you're saying, "I turned out fine. I have a good job, married, and doing well." Then there are others that are not doing so well, who also received beatings, in fact some of them end up with a history of going to jail. Receiving beatings is a form of abuse and can lead to more aggressive behavior and a greater propensity to fight than someone who didn't get beatings. It also can lead to more acts of mischief, and makes you more confrontational. By beating your daughter, it can precondition her to becoming a victim of physical and verbal abuse in her relationships. It also can contribute to her staying in an abusive relationship. I am a believer in the Bible, which says "Foolishness is bound in the heart of a child; but the rod of correction shall drive it far from him." (Proverbs 22:15, KJV). The definition of rod is a slender, thin stick. You're not going to hurt them with a slender, thin stick. The idea of disciplining is to redirect or detour the negative/bad behaviors and instill temperance, positive, and good behaviors. So get the mindset to discipline and to teach them, but don't beat them. Even though it might seem like your child is purposely doing what you told them not to do, it's not that. They're just being children. The Bible says, "When I was a child, I spoke as a child, I understood as a child, I thought as a child, but when I became a man, I put childish things away." (I Corinthians 13:11, KJV) Well at this point, they're still children, and children will be children. As adults we have to process this and deal with them as children, which means that they will be clumsy and break things, easily distracted, forget to do something that you told them to do, etc. Exercise patience, they are just being children.

Men in general don't have the patience with kids that women have. Men's patience varies drastically. Some have good patience and some have very little patience. If you don't have much patience, you need to try to learn to be patient with your children. But in the meantime, do not put yourself in situations with kids that require lots of patience, like keeping your own kids. Even if you're not working, it's better to just say no than to babysit with no patience. (This is for real, and not to be used as a cop-out.) Also if you don't have patience, don't discipline your children until you learn some, at least don't discipline with corporal punishment (e.g., spankings) because for you spankings can turn into beatings.

Next let's talk about communication. As I spoke about in the relationship chapter (see Chapter 3), communication is used at different times, in different ways, for different reasons, to get targeted results. In relationships concerning men and women, the communication needs to be two-way from the beginning and it needs to stay that way. With your children, it's different. In the beginning it's designed to be one-way. That's because to start with, they can't talk, so you have to do all of the talking. And since they come in this world not knowing anything you have to teach them everything. When they learn to talk, they're still communicating on a child's level. This is your instructional time, your guidance time, your rules and regulation time, so the communication is still basically one way. Depending on the child, when they get to age 12–15 it is extremely pertinent that the communication becomes two-way. Two-way communication means start to consider their feelings — you're still the parent and must decide what goes — but start to listen and consider. Around this time their little young lives will begin to become complicated, at least to them.

Which brings us to the teenage years, which will introduce them to a whole new world to explore. When your child comes of age, take him or her to get his or her restricted license. Set a standard for your children as far as their grades are concerned. Require that your children make exceptional grades while in grade school, and A's and B's throughout the rest of their school term until they graduate high school.

Prepare, encourage, and persuade your children to go to college. Have regular talks about it with them from about the time they start junior high school until they graduate. While your kids are young, buy them educational games and toys, as opposed to the violent video games or violent toys. As they grow, watch informational and educational television broadcasts or networks, such as the Discovery channel, the History channel, and the National Geographic channel, just to name a few. Teach your children about politics, economics, and business. Then when of age, take them to get their operator's license. Teach them about money. Teach them about credit. Teach them about a job. Communicate with them because they are going to need someone to talk to, or need *you* to talk to them. You'll later learn that your kids will not always come to you when they need to talk or have a problem. So as a parent remember you are responsible for them, so you need to go to them and get them to talk to you. Ask them questions and pry into their lives, even if they seem like they don't want to talk. Don't take it personal; it's a part of the process, but you still need to continue to ask questions and try to get them to open up and talk. That means get in their business and get to know what's going on in their lives. But to do this, you need to be a person (parent) that they can talk to. When they become a teenager, you can't make them tell you what's really going on, so you have to make them feel that they can tell you. When they get to this age, you may not believe it, but they will lie to you before they tell you what's really going on. So this is where you have to learn to listen to them, and learn where they are at in their lives, then try to understand them so you can help them. As they become young adults, you have to advise them as to what they should do. Now, keep in mind this is listening, learning, and advising. It's not swapping stories. Even though you are trying to find out what is going on with your kids, it's not wise to begin sharing your misdeeds; that can backfire and be used against you or used later to justify their actions. However you can let them know you've been where they are.

Before you know it, they are grown and you're finally finished raising them, right? Nope. That was only stage one and you're now about to enter stage two. Stage one is birth to 18 years old, that's raising them from infancy to adulthood. We've gotten them to the adulthood, and now we realize that they don't have any experience at being adults. So that means we have to now teach them at least something about being an adult. The next seven to ten years, which would be till about age 25 to 28, is a lot like teaching them some of the basics all over again. See, you taught them how to interact with children when they were children, but this time you're teaching them how to live and deal with adults. To successfully do this, you have to teach them as though they are big kids, while keeping in mind that they are young adults. Big kids because they don't know much of anything as it pertains to their new environment and responsibilities, but young adults because it's time for them to learn. In order for them to learn, you have to talk them through it and tell them what to do. You can tell them everything, in fact you should tell them everything they need to know and do. That's fine, just as long as you have them to do it. Once you talk them through the first-time adult experience, it'll be up to them from there. Teach them all about what you now know about managing and saving money, paying bills on time, being to work on time, working hard, being honest, having integrity, being a good parent, obeying the laws of the land, and establishing a good reputation. Next, we're going to talk just a little bit about a couple of specific things that apply to your son and then some things that apply to your daughter.

Chapter 6

The Role of Father to a Son: What to Teach Your Son

AS A FATHER YOU WILL find that you have a special connection to your son. Why? Because of your hormonal similarities. Testosterone plus testosterone equals male bonding. That's what's going to happen here. Your similar natures are going to lead you right into doing the things that men do with their sons: play-wrestling, play-hitting, and roughing them up. You'll start this just as soon as he can, and I'm talking as early as 3 months old. You won't be able to help it. As he grows, it'll increase to the play punches that will have more and more contact and impact. Then the intensity will continue and continue to increase; you'll be picking him up, throwing him in the air and catching him. (Moms don't do these kinda things.) You're play-slamming him on the bed, and before you know it, he is a year and a half. Around that time you will also realize that you have taught him how to hit; he now likes to hit and is hitting everyone, including other people's 1-year-olds. Of course you feel he's only doing what you taught him and because of that you really don't want to discipline him. After all, he's just being a boy. Well, before long he's in daycare, Head Start, kindergarten, and you're getting phone calls because he's still hitting. You can't defer it any longer, it's time to start the corrective process. I've coached a lot of fathers who have had a problem making this correction because they think they're going to weaken their son. But if you don't do something, you're allowing him to go on a path of aggression, which will lead to trouble that can later lead to fights and eventually incarceration. To start the correction process, give him good, clear, firm, and direct talks. Instruct him by letting him know that it's not OK to hit, push, or take things that don't belong to him. By now, you've also noticed that boys are more aggressive and tougher than girls. Therefore, boys can sometimes prove to be too much of a challenge for their mothers and need their father in their lives.

There are some other specifics that you need to teach you son(s) beyond the standard football, basketball, soccer, and baseball. Some of these may seem soft, non-essential, or anti-manly. Nonetheless, they are helpful, good to know, and necessary for general survival. You should teach your son(s) how to clean a house, wash dishes, cook simple foods, bake, barbecue, properly wash clothes, iron clothes, start a lawn mower, mow the yard, shave, blow his nose, hunt, fish, and wash a car/truck, and the importance of managing money, paying bills, and building credit, etc. Teach him about all of these things in their respective time periods. He doesn't need to know how to be a mechanic, but he should know how to do some basics, such as check and add oil, check and add water, change a battery, and change a tire.

The next thing is dating. The average age a boy begins puberty is about 11–12 years of age, and the process is normally completed around 16–17 years of age. This is the stage when he develops the desire to get to know girls up close and personal. It just so happens that she is around that same age and stage also. It is very important that you teach them how to respect young ladies. This is not going to be easy especially because it's something you probably weren't taught to do and most likely didn't do. But you need to teach him the right thing, which is to abstain from sex until marriage. It's not impossible guys. Explain to him what his body is going through, but also that sex equals children and that having children without being married greatly increases the chances of him not being there to properly raise his child, because most of those early relationships don't last or work out. This is evident by looking around at how many of their friends' mothers and fathers aren't together. Explain to him how most relationships are driven by a desire for sex. Because they didn't truly understand the real reason for their encounter, they fulfilled the nature of it, which resulted in a child. Because the male hasn't learned or developed his commitment emotion, he usually finds his way to the next attractive female, abandoning his last lover and child. It is important to stress to your son that it is always an unfair situation for a child to have to be raised without his father committed in his life, and for the young mother, who has been put through the metamorphosis of bearing a child from him, and then abandoned by him. Help him understand by telling him examples. For instance, if he had a relationship with someone, they had a child, and that particular relationship didn't work out. The same thing happened again? Finally he marries the third woman and raises the children he has with her. That would be a great situation for the kids who would see him every day, but his other children are going to miss out on a full-time father, and that's a great injustice for them, by him, and of no fault of their own. So encourage him to try to understand his sex drive, corral it, and wait until marriage so he doesn't have unplanned kids that he's not ready to take care of. This can be a hard conversation for you to have with your son, but it is a very necessary one to have.

The next thing I'm about to say may sound contrary to what I just said. If you for any reason believe that after every talk that you can think to have with your son about sex, that he is still going to have it outside of marriage, then you must have another kind of talk with him, letting him know that if he can't sustain himself, after really, really trying, and he's not ready to get married, then encourage him to use protection. I know this will be hard for the religious man to tell his son(s) because he feels like he's giving his consent to his son to fornicate. But you're not, you're just doing your job as a father and teaching your son to protect himself, the would-be mother, and the would-be child. And that's the next thing a man does besides providing, is protecting. If you don't, it would be like sending your son into a gunfight without a gun, just because you don't believe in guns. Make sure the sex is safe. I didn't say practice safe sex. If your past happens to come up, help him to understand that you didn't have anyone there to help you understand those things and that you regret the things you did. And that's why you are doing your duty as his father, in hopes that he has a better life than yours, by making sure he understands and doesn't make the same mistakes you might have made.

Chapter 7

The Role of Father to a Daughter: What to Tell Your Daughter

AS A FATHER YOU WILL find that you have a very special connection to your daughter. Your natural instinct is to protect, and her natural need is for protection. This combination is unreal and it never ever goes away. You will never understand it until you experience it. But if a man hasn't had the experience, and you give him a choice of girl or boy for his first child, if he's honest, he's probably going to say a boy. The alternative response is, "As long as it's healthy, I don't care." But he would still want to say a boy. Why? Well, it's nothing personal. Actually, it's everything personal. It's because he was a boy, and the girl on the other hand, well, she's going to grow up to be a woman — which he's still to this day trying to figure out how to understand them. Then there's also that fear factor. The fear of the unknown. Not knowing if you'll end up being incarcerated 15–30 years down the road for hurting someone of the male species for mistreating your daughter. But if he just so happens to have a girl first, second, or whenever, he will discover that he has just met the most special love of his life. She will go to a place in his heart that he didn't even know existed, a place that no one else can get to. He will feel the need to love, treasure, and protect her with his whole life, and at all times.

Your daughter will always have a very strong need in her life for her mother because of their estrogen connections, and when she goes through puberty, she is going to face the things and changes that only women go through. But then there is that very essential side of her life that even her mother cannot successfully guide her through because this problem that she's going to have, her mother still doesn't understand it herself. That essential part of her life to which I refer is her "male counterpart." It is always said that you'll never understand the ways of a woman. Well, the same holds true for the woman when it comes to men. It's not that we are complicated like women are, it's just that the level we're on is hard for women to conceive or even believe. So you bring something different to your daughter; she desperately needs her father in her life.

But first things first. As a toddler, it is important that she experiences your strength, power, and protection. As she grows through those young ages, it is very important that she experiences your presence. Of all the many things you're going to be to her and do for her, one thing that you can do better than anyone else is to arm her with the knowledge, insight, and ability to successfully face her greatest challenge: men. That responsibility is yours. That duty is yours. That job is yours. If you don't do it and do it well, you're going to send her out as a sheep among the wolves, and you know how the game goes because you were once a wolf-man yourself. So when the time comes, as a father you must arm her with your knowledge of the deceiving and misleading intentions of her male counterparts.

Your daughter actually needs both you and her mother working on her behalf as it pertains to dating and dealing with the male species. Let the mother do her part saying and teaching the things that need to come from her. As a man you know that there are things that your daughter needs to know and do, and things she shouldn't do. Some of these things are better coming from her mother, but her mother doesn't even know all of the things that need to come from her. So you will have to talk to her mother and have her talk to you all's daughter about those particular things. Then there are other things that are better coming from you, rather than her mother, so you need to talk to her about those things when it's time. No one except another male knows the real motives and intentions of a male when he approaches a female and puts on his display of genuine interest in her. You need to tell your daughter things about the thought process of a man that you didn't even tell her mother. Of course the reason you didn't tell her mother was because you were doing what a man does and saying what a man says to get with a woman. So why would you tell your daughter something that you couldn't tell other women, one of which is now your wife? Because your mission is now different than it was before. Your mission/job now is to protect the heart, emotions, and integrity of your daughter. Why do men do women the way they do them? It's just because of our primal sex drive. The man is trying to satisfy his sexual need by any means. It's like what psychologists teach as the drive reduction theory. As I stated earlier in the relationship chapter, every living thing that God created, He created it to reproduce. It's like an eco-homeostasis system. Homeostasis means to maintain a preset state. As it pertains to *homo sapiens* or human beings, the woman's reproductive drive is connected to her internal clock, which operates within a 30-day cycle. The man is primarily visually stimulated. The drive reduction theory is, when we have a need — let's say it's a physiological need like water — if the need is not met it creates a drive, which means the awareness of this need intensifies. The only way to reduce the drive is to give the body what it needs, which will be water. This is basically what happens when a man sees a woman that he's attracted to. This psychologically becomes a physiological need. The man's body creates a drive to appease this need. He then begins a pursuit, sometimes relentless, to satisfy this need. He will do whatever gets him what he wants as quickly as possible, be it lying, pretending, lying, faking, lying, or lying. This can hold true even if the male already has a sex partner. Notice earlier that I didn't say by any means necessary, and that's because the way we go about doing what we do to get what we want is not necessarily necessary. But that's what males do, and unless you thoroughly prepare your daughter, that's what he's going to do to her. So your mission/goal/job is to make her thoroughly aware of the game. Most fathers fail to do so for their daughters.

This is also your time to learn a little something about relationships as well. Remember: *We learn from our experiences, then we teach what we have learned, but the real beneficiary is he or she who learned from what they were taught.* Tell her the things that she needs to be aware of as they pertain to men and relationships. When it's time, tell her about his motive, which is sex; his goal, which is to sleep with her as soon as possible; his tactics, which are whatever it takes; and his conversation, which is to tell her whatever it is that she wants to hear. Let her know that most everything he tells her, especially how he feels about her, are all lies. You know it. You also need to tell her about what a man should do and how he really should treat her if he really cares about her the way he claims he does — like not trying to get her to sleep with him. Warn her about the reverse psychology: acting like he doesn't want to sleep with her, so it'll make her want to sleep with him because she thinks he really cares about her because she thinks he's not trying to sleep with her. During this time when you're talking to your daughter about how a guy should treat her, you may realize that some of the things you're teaching and telling your daughter, you might not be doing yourself in your own relationship. Well, allow your desire to teach your daughter how she should be treated in a relationship to inspire you to practice what you're teaching. Even though you may not be at that level, you still need to teach it to her. As you do, practice it yourself and continue to practice it until you get there. Because if you say it and don't do it, you're teaching her to have that expectation from a man. If she doesn't see it in action from you, her biological mentor, she will not really expect to receive it from the man of her interest. She will allow it to be a work in progress for him as she saw it to be a work in progress for you as it pertains to her mother.

The key to successful teaching when it comes to your kids is repetition. You have to keep teaching and telling, telling and teaching, over and over again. And remember she will also need to see it in action from you. You want to teach her these things *before* she gets in a relationship, because by then it might be a little too late. Teach her the real truth and let her know that you know, because you used to be one of those men. That's what makes you such an advantage to your daughter, because she is literally you/yours. So even though you may have been deceptive or manipulative with other women, you want to be beneficial and profitable to your daughter in every way that you can, and that's the reason you tell her that.

So your question might be, "At what age and in what manner should I go about this?" Children are people, and people, as you know, are different one from another. It just depends on your child. Now your child may start as early as age 5 when she first starts to talk about this boy at Head Start, Pre-K, or school who likes her, or whom she likes. Of course at this point, there's nothing to worry about, but it is something to think about, so you do need to be mindful of it from that point on. But at that point just respond to it on a little child's level. Ten to eleven years of age is about the average age when girls reach puberty. Be advised that they may take a more serious interest in boys around this age, give or take a year or two. Thirteen to sixteen is about the average age of real interest, but again, it depends on your child. Also note that one child may be the opposite of the other. When they get around any of the aforementioned ages just pay attention and respond accordingly. If they don't come to you, you need to go to them. Initiate some conversation on the subject. You need to create a "discussion comfort zone." Some parents make the mistake of choosing not to have these conversations because they are afraid that if they initiate this type of conversation, they're going to cause their child to start to think about something that they weren't thinking about before. Well I can assure you, just because you're not talking about it doesn't mean they're not. What it does mean is they're not talking about it with *you*.

What if the talk doesn't go right? Even though you've tried to establish the discussion comfort zone, this may still be an uncomfortable conversation. It's normal for them to shut down in this area of conversation. That doesn't mean give up. Instead, have a one-way conversation. You may do this by telling them about how the interest in dating actually begins. Don't get too involved this time around. Try to gain a little trust with them and try it again in a couple of weeks. The idea of these one-way conversations is to let them know that you know where they're at, or where they will soon be.

Some kids, once they reach this point, will choose to lie to you for no real apparent reason about what's going on in their lives. The reason they do this is because they think — or know — that you are going to disapprove, or they feel you will not understand. You must continue to talk to them in order to open the doors of communication and gain their trust. Stand by your standards, but don't be unreasonable. If you and your child don't agree, just continue to have talks regularly and try to gain their trust. But at the end of the day, you're the parent. Make the decision that's best. As a parent, you are your children's first line of defense, not their friend. Part of your job is to look for the not-so obvious, which is usually obvious. When you have discovered it, or even think you have discovered it, you need to respond to it.

So when it comes to your daughter, what are some of the things you need to do? First, watch her behavior. You should know your kid's normal behavior. That is what serves as your alarm or warning sign. When you notice that she is acting a little different, like staying in her room a lot more than normal, you need to have a no-pressure inquiry or visit her in her room. You may also discover that she is spending a lot of time on the phone or computer. You have to inquire into this matter also. Try to find out who she is talking to and what about. These conversations will first be with her other girl friends, and they will at first be talking about every little silly thing that you can imagine talking about. Then they will normally progress to talking about boys. Yes, all the boys — the geeks, nerds, ugly and cute ones. Later that will change to only the cute and "hot guys." How will you know? By listening in. Eavesdropping? Yep, that's right. When you notice her starting to talk on the phone a lot or on the computer a lot, you're going to have to get involved and investigate. That may mean you will have to listen in from time to time, or have her mother do it. Mothers usually have a natural propensity to do this. But one of you should. When she reaches certain ages and stages, she's going to try to keep certain things from you, even if it means getting angry with you and shutting down. Sometimes young girls go through a stage where everything they can do without you knowing, they will do, and also may not be truthful about where they are going and what they're doing. So there may come a time when you have to do some investigative and intrusive parenting. But your job is to know and protect them from themselves, as well as from anyone else, whether they like it or not.

The second thing you need to do is be prepared when she comes to you. If she comes to you to ask for permission to date, then you're already behind, so you will now need to deal with this with more attention and revisit this much more frequently. It's important to properly address this and not just shut it down. You may have the say-so, but she has the *do*-so. If she is not of age then discuss the age that she can start dating, which is usually about 16, but that depends on her level of maturity, and it also depends on you. But whether she is of age or not, inquire. She only asked about dating because she's already interested in someone. That usually means that they are already talking, or a friend of hers is already dating. So since she came to you, she has opened the door of communication. Begin by asking her if there is a boy who likes her. Ask what his name is, what grade he is in, how old he is, etc. After some questions about him, ask if she likes him too. Also ask her if any other boys like her, and if she likes any of them. It's very important that you do observational listening. That means observe her answers. Her body language speaks louder than her words. I would recommend trying to discourage her from dating but don't be dogmatic about it. If you just shut her down, she will make what started as a two-way conversation into a one-way conversation; she will not come to you anymore to talk. In other words, she'll eventually start dating without telling you and will not open up to you about it anymore. Definitely make the decision that you feel is best, but make her feel considered and a part of the conversation, as well as your decision. When she's of age and you do educate her on the male and his agenda, don't do it in the first or second conversation, make it a properly timed progressive event. It is also equally important for you to tell her about the qualities that make up a good woman and the things that earn her respect from a guy, one of which is saving herself. Let her know that giving in to the boy sexually is not going to keep him. In fact, it's going to help promote his interest in the next girl, to see how long it'll take him to have sex with her. Let her know that it'll just become a fun challenge for him; in the meantime she will feel used and abandoned because that's just what he will have done. But by waiting, he will still move on to the next girl, just like he would have anyway. However, this way, even though she might be disappointed, she will not feel used and abandoned. In fact guys will have more respect for her for not being like the other girls. Other qualities that make up a good woman are self-respect, education, independence, having good self-esteem, lady-like etiquette, etc. But by the same token don't give her a superiority complex disposition. Don't teach her to be a brat, such as expecting respect but not giving respect. Teach her a balance.

Chapter 8

Stepfather: Another Step in Fatherhood

THIS IS FOR ALL THE stepfathers. A stepfather is a man who marries a woman who has kids from a previous relationship(s). Her kids are hers. This is not a typo. Her kids are hers. Whether she's still raising them or they are grown and not living with her at the time, they are still hers, and just like with your kids, they may return at any time. Their home is the same as you and their mother's home. You must treat her kids as though they are your very own, as should she with yours. Also display financial, emotional, and moral support for them in whatever area they need just as you would with your kids. If they get in trouble, you need to respond with your wife (their mother) to their aid, without having to be asked. If they experience a financial need or hardship, you need to be willing to do whatever your wife would want to do, with the same consideration that you would give to your biological children. Don't try to replace their dad, but be a father figure to them. Talk to them about the things that are going on in their lives, advise them, coach them, instruct them. All of these things need to be done willingly and without having to be coerced. All of the other things that we've talked about you doing for your biological kids, do the same for your step kids. Because her kids become your kids, and your kids become her kids. Need I say that the same goes for her grandkids and your grandkids? All of you all's kids, are you all's kids.

Chapter 9

Reputation: Recreation and Restoration

"Who do people say that I the Son of man am?"
(Matthew 16:13 KJV)

E VENTUALLY A MAN'S REPUTATION WILL say more about him than he can say about himself. It will speak louder than him and get to where he's going before he gets there. Every man will have one sooner or later. It will be what you made it to be, good, bad, or in between. Or it can be what you make it to be. A reputation is a verbal report about a person's behavior that is compiled by a consensus of people who know or knew him or her. It's generated by factual, personal knowledge of your actions, deeds, and behavior over a period of time. It's official and unofficial, and yet socially accepted. In short, it's what people know and think of you. You may have asked yourself, "Should I be concerned about what people think of me? Does it even matter?" Yes, and yes. Your reputation is very important: It can help you or hurt you, make you or break you. In fact you should find out what people are saying about you; Jesus did. "Who do people say that I the Son of man am?" He wasn't talking about him the Son of God, he was talking about him the Son of man. About the life he lived right here on Earth. The way He lived his life, the things He did, and the things He didn't. You will find out that the Things you don't do have as big of an impact on your reputation as the things you do. Notice their reply. They said, "Some say John the Baptist, others say Elijah, and others Jeremiah, or one of the prophets." (Matthew 16:14 ESV) If you noticed, every report equivocated him to a prophet, who in that day and time was very highly regarded. Therefore his reputation was nothing less than impeccable. So much so that at the time of his crucifixion, because his reputation was beyond reproach, they had to pay people to lie on him in order to have a reason to put him to death. I hear people say, "They talked about Jesus so you know they're going to talk about me," but they were lying on Jesus. Are they lying on you?

You also asked whether it matters what people think or say about you. Yes, what people think of you can help you or hurt you. For example, in order to be a bishop, pastor, or deacon the Bible says "…he must have a good reputation among outsiders." (1 Timothy 3:7 HCSB) That means they must have a good reputation outside of the church as well as inside the church. But that does not only go for the minister, the Bible also tells us to "…let no one look down on you because you're young, but set an example… in your speech, conduct…" (1 Timothy 4:12 NET) God is telling you not to do stupid, silly, or bad things just because you're young and knowing that people will say, "Well what do you expect, he's young?" But God is telling you to respect yourself and live a respectful life even while you're young. When I was a young man, I became a police officer. But before the department hired me, they canvassed my neighbors and talked to the people who knew me to get their views on the kind of person I was. In other words, they were checking my reputation. I had already passed the criminal background check, but the thing about your criminal background is it only shows what you got caught doing. It doesn't tell them what you might still be doing or who you really are. So they ask the people who see you on a daily basis about that, to include your girlfriend or wife. If what the people say about you is not good, you will not get the job. So what people think about you and say about you matters, it becomes your reputation.

Your reputation starts out following you, but later it goes before you. You start out with a clean slate. Your rep isn't created until you have lived a while and done some things, good, bad, or in between. After you've started doing whatever it is that you do, people will began to talk about you. That's what people do: talk about you. When they talk about you, it'll be behind your back, not in your face: That's what people do, they talk behind your back. However, what they're saying will eventually go before you; it'll reach the people and places before you get there.

You may be thinking, If reputation is what a person thinks about me, that means it's their opinion and therefore it shouldn't be relevant, right? Well, it is relevant. Your reputation is going to be formed in one of two ways: on what people know about you, or what they heard about you, and what they heard about you usually comes from people that knew. So what it boils down to believe it or not, is that reputations are normally the truth. Rumors are speculated gossip, but reputation boils down to the truth. Anything that's not true will eventually be dismissed. Think about someone that you actually know, not someone that somebody told you about, but someone you know. Think about the things that they did that you actually know about, and I'm sure that you've told somebody about them. Other people who know things will also talk about what they know, corroborating one another's information. These different reports — good, bad, or in between — are going to become those people's reputations.

So as you live your life, the things you do or have done become a part of your past. <u>The thing about your past is, it rarely stays your past, it always finds it way into your present, and it sometimes uses that visit to change your future. When it does, it's usually not for the good.</u> As you live your life the things you do today will be your past by tomorrow and later become the history of your life. So in essence you're writing the story or history, if you will, of your life right now as you live it. The thing about history is you can't erase it once it's written. You can't change it once you've done it. But you can change what you write in the future by changing what you do right now in your present, which will become a new past therefore writing a new history. So if you will imagine with me, in essence you can rewrite your history.

You start this by changing your reputation. Once your reputation is well-established, it will be discussed at the mentioning of your name, often times by people who are yet to meet you. That's what is meant by your reputation precedes you. Your reputation has reached them before you did. Let's say for example you meet this woman and y'all start to date. She tells her friends about you and asks if any of them know you, and of course they gladly tell her anything they know: "Girl, he's a big liar," "He's a cheater," "You know he's been to jail right?" and "He has a reoccurring drug problem." It goes on and on. That's the report, because that's been your behavior. You lie a lot, you cheat, you've been incarcerated, and have a problem with drugs. Your reputation is like an audio recording of your life.

So let's talk about changing that reputation. This fix doesn't happen overnight. Think about how long you were doing the things that you were doing. The restoration/repair process works like this: Think of a video surveillance tape. Let's just say it has a two-year recording capacity. Once the tape has recorded for two years (17,520 hours), it will start to record over (rewrite) what it previously recorded, therefore erasing the old by actually replacing it with new images. Keep in mind that I used an example of two years. So that's how many old recordings or how much memory is on there. So what I want to bring to your attention is, if you only rewrite one year of new images and stop, and someone was watching that tape, the last half of what they saw would still be the old, bad, and negative stuff. Therefore, they would end up seeing your negative or bad behavior and still see you as not having changed. My point? If you start this change and halfway through it you stop, your old reputation is what's going to remain with the people. However if you complete the change, people are going to remember what they saw, which is the new you. So when you make the change, don't change back — keep going.

So to change your negative or bad reputation, which was made by negative or bad behaviors, you have to replace it with positive or good behaviors. How do you do that? You can only do that by changing yourself. You first start by acknowledging and accepting the truth about yourself. Is there any truth to what they are saying? Nine times out of ten, your reputation is true whether you want to admit to it or not. *OK, it's true. What do I do?* You start doing the opposite of what you've been doing. I know that's easier to say than it is to do; nonetheless, that's what you have to do. It is the absolute only way it can be done. Let's say your reputation came from a past lifestyle of poor judgment and acts of indiscretion, which consisted of lying, womanizing, criminal behavior, being a deadbeat dad, and having a drug problem. You first have to acknowledge and accept the truth where it applies. You must then consciously confess your change, then physically commit to the change. So let's start with being a womanizer. Acknowledge your problem: I love fine and attractive women. (Most every man does.) I love sex. (Most every man does.) Every fine or attractive woman I see I want to have sex with. (Most every man does.) Now commit to the change: Everything starts in the mind as a thought first. Before you go to apply for a job, you think about it. Before you get something to eat, you think about it. So before you meet the next fine woman that you feel you have to have, just think about it. Make up in your mind that the next woman you meet (providing you're not with one now) is going to be the one, the one you're going to stay with. When you've had this thought, and had it long enough that it has became a decision, and then a feeling, then go and find one woman to your liking and commit to her. You'll still have a desire to fool around with other women. Fight that desire, and do not give in to it. Remind yourself that you have made a decision to commit to one woman, now remain committed. Keep reminding yourself, and continue remaining committed. Soon, it will become your new nature. You also must reinforce your new change with statements of affirmation. Statements such as "I'm a changed man," "I'm not like I used to be," and "I am true to my lady," "I'm happy and I'm faithful," etc. <u>Say it, do it, and you'll be it.</u>

As it pertains to a deadbeat dad: Acknowledge, confess, and commit. Start paying your child support, then contact the mother and make arrangements to get your kid(s) and then do those other things that we talked about in the chapters pertaining to being a father. Don't do what's convenient for you. Instead, do what is right to your child. If you continue with consistency, which means without turning back, people are going to start to say, "There was a time that he didn't do anything for his kids, but now he gets them all the time." Then further down the line they'll be saying, "He's a good dad and he takes good care of his kids." See how the negative "didn't do anything for his kids" has dropped off and the whole statement is now positive? Which means that you are now living on the plus side of life.

As it pertains to lying: Stop lying. Acknowledge, confess, and commit. When the situation arises and you realize you're about to tell a lie, just stop! Believe me when I say, a liar knows that they are a liar. What you may not know is that everyone else also knows that you're a liar too; it's being talked about all the time behind your back. So to start with, stop saying things that you know you're not going to do, stop saying you did something that you didn't do, and stop saying you didn't do something when you know you did, etc. Think about what you are about to say before you say it. When you know it's about to be a lie, just stop. Make a choice to tell the truth and whatever you say you're going to do, do it. Don't change it later. If you can't do something that someone is asking of you, say it from the beginning. People will have so much more respect for you if you just tell the truth.

If you are consistent in the other areas, those areas will also change from a bad reputation to a good one. So do the same thing in all the other areas that need correcting. Acknowledge, confess, commit. If the area happens to be an area of addiction, such as drugs or alcohol, and you need additional help, then definitely seek professional counseling from someone who specializes in the area you need. But I want you to know that you can beat addictions. Acknowledge, confess, and commit.

Now if you just happen to be a young man reading this book then you've just learned that you're going to have a reputation no matter what you do. There is nothing good about a bad reputation. So take what you've read and write your reputation right, right from the start.

Chapter 10

Finances: Money Matters

"...money is the answer for everything." (Ecclesiastes 10:19, NET)

MONEY. THE THING WE HEAR about money is that it's the root of all evil. Well let's start by clarifying that. The Bible actually says, "For the love of money is the root of all evils." (1 Timothy 6:10 NET) The word love changes everything. When you love someone or something you'll do anything for them. Therefore when you love money, then that means you're willing to do anything — even bad things — to get it. On the other hand money in and of itself is a good thing, a very good thing. In fact it's a very necessary essential in and of our lives. The Bible even says " ...money is the answer for everything." (Ecclesiastes 10:19 NET) That verse tells us that money really does matter. Money is as important to our physical well-being as blood and water are. In fact contrary to popular belief, money actually can buy you happiness. My experience is that people are normally happier with money than without money. It can't buy you all of happiness, but it can buy a lot of it. Contrary to popular belief, money can buy you friends, not true friends, but it can buy you the dictionary definition of a friend, and lots of them. Contrary to popular belief, money can buy life. Not eternal life, but an extended one, one longer than you probably would have lived without it, by affording you superb health care, which is obtained by being able to afford superb health insurance. Which in turn got you additional privileged services that you would not have gotten otherwise. When the Bible says that money is the answer for everything, it means just that: everything. It is involved in every aspect of our life, and is used for every essential thing that you need, want, or desire. Let's look at a few examples of some of those needs, wants, and desires. Needs: When you get up in the mornings and turn on the light switch to see how to get dressed, those lights require electricity, and it takes money to pay the electric bill. When we brush our teeth or take a bath, that requires water. It takes money to pay the water bill. The toothpaste we use to brush our teeth, the soap we use to bathe, the clothes we put on to go to work, the lunch we fix from the food we bought, the vehicle we drive, and the gas it requires, etc. all require money. Let's look at some wants: A better vehicle, upgraded electronic devices, and some man toys, i.e. a boat and some fishing and hunting equipment, etc. all require money. Let's look at some desires: things that would be excessive or over the top, like two or three luxury cars at your disposal, the luxury boat, the excessively big house, a big closet full of all kinds of name-brand clothes, shoes, watches, cologne, perfumes, etc. Regardless of what kind of things you buy, they all require money. So money is something that we all must have, however we do not have to have all of it, or even a lot of it, but we do need to have enough of it. And although we only need to have enough to live, we should want or desire enough to live comfortably. Something else worth knowing is, money, whether it's direct or indirect, is referenced in conversation more than any other subject that we talk about. When it comes to relationship, it's going to be involved in at least 80% of the conversations. Whether it's about paying the bills, buying some clothes, getting her hair or nails done, going out to eat, to the movies on vacations, etc. The conversation is going to refer to money in some way, form, or fashion.

So make money your friend, instead of your foe. <u>Make money something you live with instead of without.</u> You can do this by creating a budget, also known as a spending plan. I'm sure you've heard the expression "people don't plan to fail, they just fail to plan." Well the first thing you need to plan to do is for you and your wife (if you're married) to plan a time to sit down and work out the budget together. The second thing you will need to do is agree on a spending plan that is reasonable and fair for both of you and your family. Third, remember, the plan will not work unless the both of you agree. So what is a budget? It's a manifest that tells you how much money you have coming in (income), and how much money needs to go out (debt/bills), and where it needs to go. A budget will help detect problem areas in your finances. It will also serve as a clear financial means of communication and accountability for both of you. What does a budget include? It needs to include all of your debts such as tithes, house payments, car loans, student loans, banks and finical institution loans, credit cards, electric bill, phone bill, water bill, cable bill, internet bill, hospital bill, etc. It also needs to include miscellaneous expenses and allotments such as hairdos, haircuts, clothes, shoes, etc. Money for entertainment and recreation such as eating out, money for going to the movies, going to theme parks, Christmas presents, vacations, birthdays, etc., you get the idea. That's a lot of stuff, and when you start to try to figure it all in a budget, most of you are going to say no way. Well that's not all, you also need to include a savings plan. The first step to savings is to stop miscellaneous spending.

Let's do a crash course on how to make all this work. Your budget is done on a month-to-month basis. You first write down all of your income and the dates it comes in. Then write all of your debts and bills down by the chronological date of the month that they are due. Take the first source of income for the month and connect it with as many of the chronological debts and bills of the month that it can handle, while allowing for gas, groceries, and enough money for personal expenses to last to the next source of income for the month. Next, we go to that next source of income for the month, and likewise pay as many of the next chronological debts and bills as you can, again allowing for gas, groceries, and personal expenses for that income period as well. Repeat this process for the rest of the month. Then repeat the entire process for each of the other months. You may discover that you're not able to get everything that we discussed above in to your budget. If that is the case, then make the necessary amount adjustments to make it work; obviously you can't adjust the amount of your debts or bills, but you can adjust the amount of everything else to make them work. Now back to that savings plan that we mentioned earlier. You definitely need to find a way to include it. If it means making sacrifices in other areas, then you need to make them. Having a savings account is very important. It's what takes care of those unexpected events also known as emergencies.

The first goal for your savings is to save an amount that's equal to one month's expenses. Do something to celebrate reaching that goal, something nice, simple, inexpensive, but meaningful. Then start on your next savings goal, which will be to save three months' worth of expenses. Do something to reward yourselves, then do six months, nine months, and finally one year's worth of expenses saved. This savings will serve as the financial transitional lifeline for you and your family in the event of an unforeseen job loss suffered by you or your spouse. Something else you should do concerning finances is try to increase your income. You may do so by seeking job opportunities in which you can advance in position and pay, without significantly sacrificing your family's quality time. You also need to be sure that you use your pay increases wisely.

Chapter 11

Good Credit: The Red Carpet or Black Top?

"A good name....rather than silver and gold."
(Proverbs 22:1 KJV)

A GOOD NAME, THAT'S WHAT GOOD credit gives you. When the Bible says a good name is rather to be chosen than great riches (Proverbs 22:1KJV), it is saying that we should work harder to get and keep a good name rather than great riches. That includes a good reputation and good credit, and since we've talked about reputation already, let's talk about credit.

Credit is a get it now, pay it later agreement between the consumer (you) and the lender/creditor, which is the provider of the cash or merchandise that we seek to obtain. Credit allows you to get the cash or merchandise (car, house, furniture, jewelry, computer, etc.) now, and make monthly payments on it until it's paid off. Credit is first established by an evaluation of your financial ability to repay a predetermined amount of money in a timely manner. The lender will then grant you the money or merchandise that was agreed upon, and will report the manner in which you repay the loan to one, two, or all three of the major financial statistical agencies called credit bureaus. These three major credit bureaus (Transunion, Equifax, and Experian) will assign a score to your credit report by using an evaluation system from one of the two financial evaluation agencies called credit scoring bureaus. The two credit scoring bureaus are FICO (Fair Isaac Corporation), and Vantagescore. FICO scoring is used by 90% of the lenders, however Vantage scoring, which came on the scene in 2006, is gaining momentum.

Your lenders send a detailed report to each of the credit bureaus. The three credit bureaus each assign you a credit score based on the evaluation systems of the two credit scoring bureaus, which are similar. These scores are based on several different things, such as payment history, current level of debt, longevity of your credit history, and available credit. FICO scoring, which ranges from 300–850, has eight (8) ratings:

1. exceedingly poor 300–499
2. very poor 500–549
3. poor 550–599
4. fair 600–649
5. good/average 650–699
6. really good 700–749
7. excellent 750–799
8. incredibly good 800–850

Vantage score, which ranges from 501–990, has (5) ratings:
1. F= 501–600 You may not be eligible for a loan.
2. D= 601–700 You may qualify, but the interest rates will be very high.
3. C= 701–800 You may qualify for the loan, but not at a good interest rate.
4. B= 801–900 There won't be any problem getting a loan at a good interest rate.
5. A= 901–990 The lender will offer you their best interest rate.

The better your credit, the more you get and the less you pay. This is the difference between good credit and poor credit. Let's just say you went to a dealership to buy a car. One of the first things the salesman is going to try to do is ascertain a verbal financial assessment from you. He's going to want to know where you work, how much you can put down, and what you can afford to pay a month. Then he is going to pull your credit history to see what kind of credit risk you are. If you happen to have excellent credit, and so choose to, you could say that you work for so and so and you want to get that Lexus LS 460 and you don't want to put any money down. He's going to think, *Yeah, right, sure you do*, but he's going to say, "Excellent choice sir, let's go inside. I need to get a little bit of information from you, and we'll go from there." All he really needs at this point is your social security number. We all add up to, or round down to, numbers, whether it be a social security number or a credit score number. Once your 835 FICO credit score comes back, he'll then say to you, "Sir, we can certainly put you in that car with absolutely no money down and we can do that today!" and they do it. Now let's look at the same scenario, but instead of having excellent credit, you have poor credit. This time he comes back with your FICO score of 547, which would actually be considered very poor credit, and he says, "Sir we are unable to put you in that car because of your credit rating, but we do have another vehicle that I'm sure you'll like just as much," which of course, you won't. What it comes down to is the amount of money the lender is willing to trust you to pay back. An excellent credit history tells the lender that you always pay back and that you're always on time with your payments. A poor credit history tells the lender that you don't repay your debt as agreed and that you often times don't pay it back at all. So therefore if they loan you money, which they may not, it will only be a small amount.

Let's take a look at a financial comparison. Let's say you wanted to buy a car that cost $20,000 (tag, taxes, and title included), and you wanted to pay for it over five years. With excellent credit your interest rate can be as low as 1% (in some cases 0%). Your payments for five years would be around $341 a month. Same scenario but with poor credit, your interest rate could be between 18–28%. Let's do 22%: Your monthly payments on the same vehicle would be $552. That same vehicle would cost you $12,660 more because of your poor credit. On a $35,000 vehicle, with excellent credit your monthly payments would be $598, with poor credit $997 a month. This vehicle would cost you $24,000 more. That's the price of another vehicle. Now let's consider a house. The amount is $150,000 with excellent credit at 2% over 30 years; your monthly principal payments would be $554 (escrow not included). Having poor credit would force you to have to finance that same house at a higher rate, at like 7% or even higher. Let's do 7%: Financing that house at 7% because of poor credit instead of 2%, your monthly payments would be $997 (escrow not included). Over 30 years, you would pay nearly one hundred and sixty thousand dollars ($159,480) more for that house than your neighbor with good credit. $160k more. That's hard to fathom. With bad credit, you would also be required to put thousands down on your loan, and in the case of the house, tens of thousands of dollars down. In the case of the excellent credit, you would be required to put very little or no money down. Now that we know what credit is, and what it does, let's talk about how to establish it.

The only way to establish credit is to obtain money or merchandise from a lender, such as a bank or place of business that reports to the credit bureaus. So when doing business to establish credit, ask the lending institution if they report to the credit bureaus. If they do not, then go somewhere that does. McDonald's, Hooters, or Red Lobster does not report to the credit bureaus. So no matter how many of thousands of dollars you spend there, you're not establishing any credit. There are a lot of other places that don't report to the credit bureaus, such as "Buy Here Pay Here" car lots, rent-to-own centers, etc. If you're just starting out, then you have no credit. No credit is not poor credit. No credit simply means you don't have a credit history and no one has ever loaned you any money. That means in order for you to get anything (e.g., a car, apartment, or furniture), you're going to need what is called a co-signer. Having a co-signer means that someone with good credit has to sign on the loan with you. I don't recommend being a co-signer, but if you do it, only do it for your kids, and only to get them started. As a co-signer you're actually saying that you are responsible for the entire loan if the borrower doesn't pay it back. So that's not a predicament you want to be placing yourself in.

If you're just starting out and don't have a co-signer then you will need to build your credit yourself from scratch. Here's how you do it: First you have to save between $300–$500. Go to a bank or credit union (credit unions usually have less maintenance fees), and ask to open a secure credit or savings account. Nowadays banks and credit unions run credit checks on you, and if you have bad credit they will not allow you to open an account there. But if you let them know that you want to open a secure account for the purpose of building credit, they will accommodate you. (Restrictions may apply). The way this works is you will give them cash money, which they will put in an account to hold as collateral, and give you a credit card or hard cash with a credit line equaling the same amount of cash that you gave them. I would recommend you put in between $300–$1,000. It would be even better if you did two secured lines of credit, one as a credit card, the other as a savings account, each for $300–500. The beauty of this is you get to use this money just as you were going to use it before, except now it's building your credit and you're doing it on your own without a co-signer. If you put in $1,000, they would give you a credit card or hard cash back (or both) with a $1,000 line of credit. They will send you a monthly statement (a bill), and you pay that amount each month, on time. This is how you build credit. Do this for a year without being late on any of your payments, and as you pay the credit card or the savings account down, you can reuse the money. Make sure you make every payment before its due date. To maximize the building of your credit, do not charge or use more than 30% of your credit card line of credit. That shows the creditor that you have control and can manage money. On the other hand, if you constantly max out your credit card(s), it tells the creditors that you spend everything you get, which sends the message that you may be a credit risk. After a year, pay your accounts off, then apply for a nonsecure loan. This means that they will look to see that you paid your bills on time and paid the secure loan off. Based upon satisfactory findings they will give you a nonsecure loan, which means they would return your money back to you and loan you their money. Now you are on your way. Other credit institutions will now loan you money, or merchandise on credit. If you continue to make your payments on time, eventually your line of credit will reach enough for you to purchase your dream home of $250,000 or more. There's a lot more to learn, but for now, that's enough information to get you on the road for establishing excellent credit.

Now what about restoring bad credit? Your credit may be in ruins because you lost your job, or because you got in over your head and couldn't pay your bills due to frivolous spending. No matter what the cause was, you can correct it. You start the process by calling 1-877-322-8228 or going online to www.annualcreditreport.com and getting your free annual credit report. This one number gives you access to all three credit bureaus. You get one free credit report a year from each credit bureau and you can make your request to each of them during this one call. It is necessary to get a credit report from each credit bureau because creditors don't always report your credit history to all three bureaus. So you may have a bad report in one bureau that's not in the other two. And each credit bureau will give you a different credit score. When the lender pulls your credit report, they usually go with the score in the middle. They use that one as an average. It takes up to three weeks to get your report.

In the meantime you need to get on a budget, which is also called a spending plan, and keep a written manifest of your income versus your expenses. Then stop spending spontaneously on unnecessary things, and you will actually discover that you have started to save just by doing that. Next, start making sure you pay all your bills on time. Pay a little extra on your smallest bill until you get it paid off. When you get that bill paid off, take all the money you were paying on that bill, including the extra, and pay it on the next smallest bill. By repeating this process, you will eliminate your credit cards and loans debt. Once you've paid them off, you may continue to use them just use them responsibly.

When you've done this, or while you're doing this, look through all three of your credit reports. Write down all of your unpaid debts on a separate piece of paper. Sometimes all three credit bureaus will show the same unpaid debt, so you only need to write it down once. Sometimes one of the three bureaus will show an unpaid debt that the other two don't show. That's normal and that's why you need all three reports. Once you've written down all the unpaid debts, you may call the phone number associated with that debt to arrange a payoff. Only call one at a time, wait until you've paid that debt off before calling the next. Starting with the smallest, work your way up. The debt collectors that you speak to can take off up to 50% of that unpaid debt, but they cannot offer the settlement, so you have to ask. Whenever they agree to do that, you have a limited amount of time to pay it off.

This process takes a little bit of time. But starting this process is the start of rebuilding your credit.

Settling the unpaid debt in the credit reports is when your score increases the most. If you need additional help, you may contact me at asktonygsr@yahoo.com , or another professional financial planner to further assist you on a plan that will work for you.

Chapter 12

Driver's License: Pilot or Passenger?

BELIEVE IT OR NOT THERE are a lot of men out there who do not have a driver's license. Some are young men who just haven't gone to get theirs yet. Some are young men who have gotten tickets for driving without a license and now have fines to pay. Some men have a license that has been suspended or revoked for traffic violations. As a result some have to pay hefty fines to get their license reinstated, and some have to wait for a court-determined amount of time before they can get their license back. Then there are the men who have a valid driver's license, but are committing traffic offenses and have yet to be caught, but once caught it could cost them their license. Whether you've never had a license, or have lost your driving privileges, you're in a counterproductive situation. Not only are you in a counterproductive situation, you become a hindrance to those around you because they have to stop or alter what they are doing in order to accommodate you. It's not important how the loss of your driving privilege came to be, what is important is that you rectify it.

A driver's license has a huge impact on your life. It plays a major role in whether you get a job or are able to keep a job, because in most cases you need transportation to get or keep a job, and if you have transportation you have to have a license to legally drive your transportation. If you have a girlfriend or wife, she's going to be terribly inconvenienced. By the way, when I coach women on relationship, I tell them, "If a man doesn't have a job, transportation, or a license, don't date him." Not having a license has caused you to force the lady into your role and you into hers. When y'all are going out, she has to pick you up instead of you picking her up. The whole while y'all are dating she has to do all the driving, she doesn't get a break. If you have a job, then whenever she's available she's has to take you to work and pick you up and take the kids everywhere they have to go with no help from you. Then if you do start to slip and drive, even if it's trying to take some of the load off her, if you get caught (and you will eventually) you're either going to jail or paying fines, which is going to create another hardship. So I encourage you to do whatever you need to do to get your license.

If you've never had one, then just go to the driver's license bureau in your area, get a driver's license book, study it thoroughly, then return there, and take the test. If you have a driver's license that's suspended or revoked, you can get them reinstated by satisfying the violations. The violation(s) are usually going to be a fine, or fines, resulting from a traffic infraction(s). Some suspensions or revocations may require that you wait a certain amount of time before your license can be reinstated. Whatever it is, do not complicate the matter more by getting additional charges added on to what you already have, because then it could turn into jail time, which could cost you your job and create a hardship on your family.

Chapter 13

A Job: Production Line or President?

"If any will not work, neither let him eat." (2 Thessalonians 3:10)

IT'S A MUST THAT A man has a job. Notice that that scripture says "him," neither let "him" eat. If an able-bodied man will not work then don't feed him. You're expected to be able to support yourself financially, and if you create a family you need to be able to support them also, or at least be a significant part of their support. This means getting a job if you don't have one. These might not be the best of times economically speaking. At the time of this book our economy had taken a big hit and men and women who have had jobs for 10, 20, or 30 years suddenly found themselves out of work. Under such conditions, it is understandable if you don't have a job. However, it still is a requirement, and believe it or not, there are still jobs out there and some good jobs at that. How do you go about getting one of these jobs?

The first thing is to seriously apply yourself. Now in doing this, you need to analyze your situation. You may or may not have transportation. We'll talk about that in a minute. If you don't have transportation, then I recommend that you start your job search at places as close to your home as possible (e.g., in walking distance or in bike riding distance). If you are not able to find anything in that range, then begin to work your way out. A lot of cities now have a bus transportation system. If your search goes beyond walking or riding a bike, and you are going to have to rely on the bus for your mode of transportation, there are a couple of things you should do. First, know all the bus schedules at the places you're seeking employment. Before any establishment hires you, they are going to want to know that you have a dependable means of transportation to get to work. So if you have to use the bus system to get to work, then you need to know their pickup and drop-off times so you can reference this as a means of transportation. Given a work schedule that complies with one of your bus schedules, the second thing you need to do is confidently assure your potential employer that you will be a reliable employee. If you have to rely on the bus for your transportation, then make sure you don't miss it. You may ask a friend or family member for a ride from time to time, and that may start out OK, but friends and family have proven to be an unreliable source of transportation.

For various reasons, the job most people start out working will not be the type of work they would have preferred to do. In fact most people work their entire life, and never do the work they would have preferred. It could have been because they weren't qualified to do the kind of work they wanted to do, it was too far to travel, or maybe they never figured out what kind of work they really wanted to do. What they did know however is that the work that they were doing wasn't it. So it may be necessary to accept the job, whether it's the kind of work you want to do or not. But remember you don't have to stay where you start. When doing a job that you don't desire to do, allow it to inspire you to do better. Allow it to make you better, not bitter. Sometimes when you're doing something you don't want to do, it can reveal to you what you'd rather be doing. It may be to become team leader or to become the manager of that company. From there you may be inspired to become the CEO/president of your own business, and from there who knows — maybe become president of the United States of America. Whatever it is, when you realize it, go for it. You may have to go back to school to get some additional training, education, or a degree in a particular field in order to complete that desire. Remember; _**if you don't do what you need to do to be what you desire to be, then you will have to be what someone else tells you to be.**_ However in the meantime, whatever job you're working on, make sure you work hard and do a great job. Always be to work on time every day, and don't call in to take off when you are on the schedule to work. Always work hard and smart without complaining, no matter what your co-workers are doing. Learn your job to the utmost, and do it well, then start to think in terms of moving up to the next position. Continue to do this until you reach the top. If a better job comes available in the company or with another company, then apply for it. If you get the job, be sure to put in your two weeks' notice with your current job and then move on. When working a job, learn about all of your benefits including retirement, stocks, and deferred compensation packages. Get into these programs early and use these benefits to their fullest potential, even if it means making some financial sacrifices in other recreational areas. These sacrifices will really pay off down the road at a time when you really need it.

Now, let's say you have a different kind of problem. You have a criminal past, including some felony convictions. You now realize that your past is hindering your future. Because of your background, employers don't want to hire you. What can you do? Well, I've coached many men with criminal records, some being quite extensive. In these cases where you can't get anyone else to hire you, I suggest you hire yourself. That's right, hire yourself. Here, I help my clients identify their gifts, goals, or talents, then instruct them on how to turn that gift or talent into a business. I teach them how to become an entrepreneur, how to set up the business, where to set it up, how to hire motivated employees, teach business etiquette, employee-customer relations, and much more. It doesn't matter what everybody else is doing, who all lost their jobs, or what the economy says. What does matter is what you think, what you give, what you do, and what you say. There are many untapped entrepreneurship's just lying dormant in most people. You just have to know how to tap into it. Once you discover your gift, talent, or passion, commit to it and invest in it. Once you start your business, take heed to the business and benefits tips we discussed above (look into IRAs, 401(k) etc.) and you will do fine.

Chapter 14

Transportation: Getting Where You Need to Go

EVERY ABLE-MINDED AND -BODIED MAN needs to have his own transportation. Transportation does not only represent your physical means of transport, it subliminally represents your inner propensity to succeed or lack thereof. My statement isn't based on the type of vehicle you drive, nor the price of it. It's about mindset; it's strictly about having transportation or not having transportation. The transportation or lack thereof is an indicator of your mindset. The man who has the mindset to get transportation, in a sense has laid a foundation of independence and has psychologically liberated himself to go places and to create his own path. He has given himself choices. The man that aspires not to obtain his own transportation has of his own volition (will) physically and psychologically resigned himself to a state of dependency and lack of achievement. He tends to struggle more and accomplish less. He will find himself living with others and having to move about from one place to another. He may also have trouble getting and keeping a job and trouble establishing himself.

The other thing you do by not challenging yourself to get a vehicle is compromise your position as a man. The same inconveniences, interruptions, and hardships that you impose on family, friends, and loved ones by not having a driver's license, are the same inconveniences, interruptions, and hardships you impose on them by not having transportation. The two are basically one and the same. Not having a driver's license means you can't drive (legally), not having any transportation means you can't drive (literally). When you get in a relationship, your lady always has to come pick you up and take you everywhere you have to go; that's not the way it's designed to work. Again, transportation in and of itself is not about the type of vehicle that you drive, but about having a vehicle to drive. So with that said, let's look at how to get some starter transportation.

First you have to save the down payment, begin with a savings goal of about $500–$1,000. When you reach $500, look at what's available, but the longer you can wait, work, and save, the better the choice of transportation you will have. Buying from an individual usually gets you a better vehicle at a cheaper price than at roadside "Buy Here Pay Here" car lots. Once you have decided on a vehicle, take it to a mechanic and get it checked out before you purchase it. From this point you can continue to work, save, and get better and better things in the future without creating financial burdens for yourself. Also keep in mind that once you purchase a vehicle, you have to purchase and maintain a tag and insurance on it.

Here's something you don't want to do as it pertains to getting a vehicle. Don't let your want get in the way of your need. Don't take your money that you've saved up to buy a good, dependable vehicle and become enticed to buy what your friends or "frenemies" have, or start yearning to get what's popular, what's cool, or attractive, because that would end up putting you in a lot more debt and a situation that's hard to afford or maintain. Which usually means that you will not have money to do the other things that you need to do, like pay bills or take care of other family responsibilities. So I advise you to start out with something that won't take all of your money. It may not be the vehicle you want, but it's only temporary. This will allow you to do other things that you need to do and save money for your more desired vehicle down the road without causing financial hardships along the way.

Remember what we talked about earlier. If you're in a relationship and your partner has a vehicle, that doesn't negate the fact that you still need your own. Even if you're married and living in the same household you will still need to get another vehicle, but you can plan for it, and get it according to the plan.

Chapter 15

Diploma or GED: Get Your Papers

LAST BUT NOT LEAST, FOR all the men out there who do not have a diploma or GED, you really should apply yourself and get one. You probably feel like you don't need it if you've already passed that time in your life when you were supposed to have gotten it, especially if you already have a job and/or a significant amount of time has already passed. But there may come a time, for some unforeseen reason that you have to find another job, or you just want a better job, and fate would have it that the next/other job require proof of your diploma or GED. There may come a time when you may be trying to tell your children of the importance of having one. You will be much more able to convey this point if you actually have your own, and last but certainly not least <u>it's just better to have it and not need it, than to need it and not have it.</u>

To get one you can go online and look up the nearest adult school in your area. They also have what are called "Drop Back In" programs for those who may have dropped out of school for whatever reasons. This program allows you to drop back in, and get the education and preparation you need to get your diploma or GED. If you're older and prefer it, there's also adult school that you can go to and get the same results.

Well, I hope this book has been a help to you. I wish you success and that you will be blessed.

Note from the Author

I pray that this book will help you become a better man, a better husband, a better father, and a better person (uncles, nephew, cousin etc.). Make your home a better place, your neighborhood a better place, your community a better place, your city a better place, and your county a better place, Become a legend, and leave a legacy. Change begets change. God bless you.

Dedication

THIS BOOK IS DEDICATED TO
ALL MY GRANDKIDS

TONY ALLEN GASKINS III
TAYDEN ANTHONY GASKINS
PRINCESS AMIAH GASKINS
TALIYAH AMARE GASKINS
ALLEN FRANK BRINSON
KYRIE ASTON BARNES
ELI ALAN ABRAM
JORDYN LAYSHY ABRAM

Special Thanks

I want to give a special thanks to my wife Vannant Baker Gaskins, my daughter Latesha Vontrice Gaskins, and Cathy Gaskins for their proofread feedback. To my son Tony A Gaskins Jr for his facilitating this book through the course of editing, formatting, ebook, and graphics. I'm thankful to you all.

www.ingramcontent.com/pod-product-compliance
Lightning Source LLC
Chambersburg PA
CBHW060159050426
42446CB00013B/2902